HOW TO FIND A JOB IN NORWAY

INGRID ROMUNDSET FABRELLO
DAVID NIKEL

WORDS OF NORWAY

HOW TO FIND A JOB IN NORWAY

First Edition. July 2018.

Copyright © 2018 David Nikel and Ingrid Romundset Fabrello.

Published by Words of Norway.

ISBN (Print Edition): 978-82-691307-1-3

ISBN (Digital Edition): 978-82-691307-0-6

CONTENTS

Welcome to Norway!

Whether you've lived here for years, you've just arrived, or you're still planning the big move, this book will guide you towards finding the job that will help to build and sustain your new life in Norway.

Living in Norway is a dream for so many people around the world, and rightly so! The country has so much in its favour and regularly features in the upper reaches of charts for such attractive things as standard of living, happiness, and working conditions.

Yet there are challenges to the process. The biggest barrier for almost any non-Norwegian considering a move to Norway is finding suitable employment.

As a native English speaker new to Norway, finding a job in which fluency in Norwegian is not a pre-requisite can be incredibly difficult. Even when you've learned Norwegian to a casual everyday level, finding employment in the country as a foreigner can still be a challenge.

But it's a challenge that can be overcome! Many foreigners find suitable employment and go on to lead happy and fulfilled lives here in Norway. In this book, we're going to show you how.

We wrote this book to share our combined experience on this challenging topic. One of us is Norwegian and one of us is not, which means you get the perspective both of an insider and from someone who's been through the process of job seeking as a foreigner. To give some context to our advice, here's a little bit about each of us.

INGRID ROMUNDSET FABRELLO

Hello everyone. My name is Ingrid, and I'm the Norwegian.

I was born and raised in Orkanger, a small town close to Trondheim in central Norway. I have always been fascinated by people and social patterns, and when I moved abroad to Nicaragua to study Spanish, I realised that my true passion was to understand social codes and their cultural differences. Many times, the cultural codes that seem to separate us from each other and make us feel different, can, once "culturally translated" show us that we all around the world have the same base motivations in what we do; we all want to feel loved, safe and connected. I hope that this book can contribute to your understanding of Norwegian culture and thus make you feel more included and at home here!

After my studies in Nicaragua, I went on to get a master's degree in social anthropology at NTNU, Trondheim's university. And after living, studying and working in the United States and in Argentina, I moved back to Trondheim with my Argentinian husband in 2011. By accompanying my husband in the process of being a foreign job seeker in Norway, I realised through his trial and errors that many people would benefit from a guiding hand once they start their relocation to Norway. In 2014 I therefore started my own company, Kulturkoordinator, which aimed to help foreign job seekers find a job in Norway. Many of my clients were the husbands, wives or partners of people who'd been transferred by their current employer, or found a professional job in a major company.

Unlike their husband, wife or partner who walks straight into a social network and support system, these so-called "trailing spouses" have none of that, and can often struggle to settle. Although I did help in finding job placements and work experience opportunities, the main purpose of the business was to offer training workshops and one-to-one counselling to help people help themselves.

Since 2014, the business helped more than one hundred foreign job seekers in and around the Trondheim region.

I've since moved on to other projects, and am currently working as an employment specialist at Euroskolen here in Trondheim. Even though I no longer run Kulturkoordinator, I desperately wanted to capture the experience and learnings from those years so that other people can benefit in the future. I chose to write this book with David to share that knowledge with you.

DAVID NIKEL

Hello everyone. My name is David, and I'm the foreigner.

I moved to Norway from the UK back in 2011 to take up a

temporary position in the ICT industry. I made the most of that time by travelling the country extensively and really getting to know Norway and Norwegian culture. Within a year, I'd decided that I liked it here and wanted to stay. My job search began! A few months later, I joined a small Norwegian software company as a consultant.

Fast forward to 2018 and I now work for myself as a writer and consultant to Norwegian businesses. I also run a small publishing company. Our most well-known publication is Life in Norway, a website, newsletter and podcast that reaches more than one million people in Norway and all around the world every year. Its aim is to help native English-speakers - or those who use English as a bridging language - find out what life in Norway is really like. Running the site has given me a unique insight into the struggles of my fellow foreigners living here in Norway. Every single day I receive emails and without doubt the number one enquiry is about finding a job.

I met Ingrid at a co-working space in Trondheim shortly after she launched Kulturkoordinator, and we instantly hit it off. Her business was an ideal match for my audience, and I was able to refer several people to her program. She wrote a guest article for Life in Norway, which proved to be incredibly popular. It was read and shared by English-speakers seeking work all across Norway, and also by people in other countries who were considering making the move.

This was the lightbulb moment for the both of us. Ingrid's business could only help a limited number of people in the immediate vicinity of Trondheim, but I had an audience of thousands all around the world who could benefit from her sound advice. Over the next few months, we debated the best way to make this happen. The book you are reading now is the result!

HOW TO USE THIS BOOK

This book is structured a little differently from what you may be used to. We wanted to create a practical guide to finding a job, and that meant approaching the writing process a little differently.

Ingrid has experience as a recruitment counsellor, and has helped many foreigners find work and adapt to working culture in Norway. As a native Norwegian, she knows what her fellow citizens look for in a potential employee, and what their concerns are when faced with a foreigner, new to Norway, who is still learning the language and the customs of the country.

David has experience as moving to Norway as a native English-speaker. He knows how difficult it can be to seek out job opportunities, especially while you don't yet have a grip on the language and lack a professional network. During his years in Norway, he's also learned a lot about Norwegian working culture, including what to do and what not to do.

So, we wrote individual chapters in our areas of expertise. During the writing process, David held a survey of Life in Norway readers who were currently working in the country. You'll see statistics from the survey and some of the comments we received sprinkled throughout the book to illustrate the challenges and our solutions.

We also include links to online resources that can help clarify and/or provide further reading about a specific topic.

Before looking at specific strategies and tactics for job hunting, David begins by taking a deep-dive into Norwegian working culture. As you'll come to learn, it's so important to understand what is different about a Norwegian workplace to avoid wasting time in the job hunt.

As you'll learn from Ingrid, a Norwegian job interview is just as much about your potential employer wanting to see if you'll be a good fit into their office dynamic than it is about your skills or experience.

We then take a look at the top employers in various sectors to help point you in the right direction if you already have a good idea about the kind of job you want to do. We also look at small employers, which can often provide great opportunities for newcomers.

Ingrid then takes us through the meat on the bones of this book, with specific tips and advice on finding a job in Norway. She talks about the differences in the job search online versus in person, and the unquestionable importance of committing to learning the Norwegian language to fluency. She also outlines what a Norwegian employer expects to see from a CV/resume.

We then discuss the Norwegian job interview, which can be very different from what you are used to. Don't let all that hard work of securing an interview go to waste by not knowing what to expect.

Ingrid has also included a couple of interviews with foreigners who successfully found a job in Norway following her program, while David offers up some tips for those wanting to start a business. Whether you want to run a business long-term or you just plan to work freelance while you search for a job, this is handy information to have.

How you use this book is up to you. It can of course be read cover-to-cover, or you might find it equally useful to dip in and out for the advice that is most relevant to you at the moment you need it.

Whoever you are, and wherever you currently live, we wish you all the best with your job search here in Norway.

Are you ready?

- Ingrid and David

CHAPTER TWO
WORKING CULTURE

DAVID

If you've not yet committed to moving to Norway, it's worth taking some time to understand the country's unique culture, and how this impacts the workplace.

It comes as a shock to many foreigners just how relaxed Norwegian office culture can be, especially those making the move from workaholic cultures like the USA.

But relaxed is not the same thing as lazy. Despite short working hours, generous holiday allowances, a consensus-based decision-making system and informal dress codes, Norwegian offices are some of the most productive in Europe, according to recent research.

The second annual Global Productivity report from B2B marketplace Expert Market investigated productivity levels in over 35 countries and found Norway to be the overall winner in Northern Europe, and ranked in second place behind only Luxembourg when it came to Europe as a whole.

I won't dig into the details of that survey here, but clearly there's something to the Norwegian model that works.

Not only will the information in this chapter help you decide whether or not to pursue a career in Norway, it should also help you to prepare for the job application and the interview process. These will both be different from what are you used to in your home country, so being prepared for these differences will help you perform better, and ensure you make the most of your time.

If you don't show an appreciation for the elements of working in Norway that are discussed in this chapter, it will come across in your interview and lessen your chances of being seen as a good fit for the organisation.

Of course, the information here is absolutely a generalisation. There is no such thing as a typical Norwegian office, and if you work in a high-pressure environment such as a restaurant kitchen or a cleaning company, you may find that only a few of these apply, if any.

That said, working with Norwegians will be so much easier if you understand these basic principles and some of the reasons why Norwegians behave the way they do.

Now, make a cup of tea or coffee, get comfy, and come with us on a walk around a typical Norwegian workplace.

Useful resources:

- Podcast - Working Culture in Norway:
  https://www.lifeinnorway.net/episode4/

EQUALITY

Norway ranks #1 in the world for equality according to the Human Development Index, a result of many years of work by successive government.

Steps have been taken to ensure men and women have equal access to higher education, along with equal opportunities to access jobs and in the choice of occupation. Today, women's participation in the Norwegian labour market is among the highest in Europe.

Broadly speaking, today's women and men enjoy equal levels of education, while the numbers of women in the workplace have increased dramatically since the 1960s.

Work is still ongoing though, and some challenges do remain. More men work in the private sector while more women work in the public sector, something that contributes to the average income for a woman being around 85% that of a man simply because private sector pay tends to be higher.

This inequality is also related to the lower numbers of female entrepreneurs, and that men hold many of the key political, economic and other decision-making positions. Religion, culture and sports are all areas which present ongoing challenges to gender equality.

A FLAT HIERARCHY

Norwegians are not fans of middle management. Small groups or teams are commonplace, yet it is rare to find much of a formal, hierarchical management structure in place.

Typically, team leaders liaise with management, but decisions within groups are taken by consensus.

While job roles are often named 'junior', 'senior' and so on, in practice these make little difference to day-to-day duties beyond the salary. This is also reflected in the open-plan offices used by many companies. The first time you walk into a Norwegian workplace, it can be very difficult to work out who is the boss just from the office layout.

SOFT LEADERSHIP

Those who do end up in a management position tend to lean towards a soft leadership style.

Soft leadership is one that emphasises soft skills and personal development over a task-focused approach. To have a boss with a soft leadership style can be a big challenge for someone who is used to being told what to do.

Soft leaders also tend to avoid conflict wherever possible. Mistakes are discussed and learned from in an open, constructive way, rather than by playing the blame game.

This means that on occasion you must learn to bite your tongue. Raising your voice in a meeting is almost never acceptable.

FORMALITY, OR A LACK OF

Unless your job is a customer-facing role, there's generally no need to dress formally for a Norwegian office job.

During the winter, it's common to have a room or area set aside for removing wet, thick winter clothing and boots, and to change into something more comfortable. Don't be surprised to see your colleagues walking around the office in trainers, slippers, socks or even going barefoot!

Some other elements of the informal workplace you may come across are a communal cake or some other sweet treat on a Friday, which you will probably be expected to buy when it's your turn on the schedule. The same applies on your birthday. Unlike in many other countries, it's you who will be expected to buy the cake for your birthday, and not your colleagues!

Some offices hold informal raffles for a bottle of wine or something similar once a month. Although informal, your colleagues will not be impressed if you decline to participate.

MEETINGS

Norwegian meetings are quite distinctive and can take some getting used to. There is rarely a formal agenda, and it is common for them to be structured to promote discussion and so that everyone can have their say. Norwegian managers value the input of everyone, and decisions are often taken by consensus rather than on the say-so of one person.

I remember clearly one of the very first meetings I was involved in. The discussion was quite technical in nature and not something I knew a great deal about. Even though I was new and involved only from the project management side of things, I was asked for my opinion.

After a rabbit in the headlights moment, I hesitated, and said that my opinion wasn't relevant given that I was so new and didn't fully understand the context of the project. Yet the person running the meeting insisted.

I thought this so strange, yet what I found even more strange was discussing it with my new Norwegian colleagues later at lunch. They had absolutely no idea what I was talking about, while my new international colleagues just sat there smiling.

Of course, decisions are unlikely to be taken on the input of someone who doesn't fully understand the topic. The point is that Norwegians feel it is important that everyone should have their say, even if it can lengthen the decision-making process.

While this can take some getting used to, especially for technical experts, I do see the benefits of this approach. It helps to create a more harmonious working environment, where no-one is worried about speaking up or sharing their ideas or concerns.

TIMELINESS

Be on time for job interviews, meetings and any appointment with a Norwegian. If you are even just a couple of minutes late it will be noticed, and it will be remembered.

It's hard to shake off a reputation for tardiness, so if you are coming from a culture where timekeeping is less important, this should be a priority for you to work on. You'll read more about this topic later in the chapter on job interviews.

WORK-LIFE BALANCE

There are very few jobs in Norway with working hours longer than 37.5 hours. In addition, many people arrive at work early most days so they can leave early on a Friday, or simply to get more work done before others arrive and the meetings start. As a rule of thumb, provided you are getting your work done, the actual number of hours you sit at your desk is not really monitored.

Life priorities to a Norwegian include their families and especially their children, and spending time playing sports or simply enjoying the outdoors. All these things are more important than work. Norwegians absolutely work to live and not the other way around.

As such, don't be at all surprised if many of your colleagues vacate the office by 2pm on a Friday to drive to their mountain cabins. The importance of children in Norwegian society is also reflected by complete acceptance for parents leaving early to fetch their children from kindergarten, or to stay at home if their children are sick.

Undoubtedly one of the biggest perks of being an employee in Norway is the entitlement to parental leave. The system in Norway is generous and flexible, as it entitles the mother and father to share the workload.

You are eligible for parental benefits if you have been employed with a pensionable income for at least six of the 10 months prior to the start of the parental benefit period. The total benefit period for a birth is 49 weeks at 100 percent coverage, or 59 weeks at 80 percent coverage, with complex but generous rules about how this can be split between the parents.

Vacations are also generous. By law, all employees must be given 20 holiday days, in addition to the annual public holidays such as Labour Day (1 May) and the Constitution Day (17 May). Many employees are given 25 holiday days, plus the public holidays.

A FOCUS ON EDUCATION

Education is highly valued in Norway. A commitment to continuous professional development is expected and actively encouraged at all levels of an organisation from senior leadership to office administrators.

For many professional jobs, a Master's degree is the minimum level of education to give yourself a fighting chance of securing an interview. That's because a very high proportion of Norwegians study their chosen field through to Master's level, mainly because of the free tuition fees in the country.

If you only have a Bachelor's degree, you will have to show exceptional skills and experience, and a commitment to furthering your professional qualifications to stand an equal chance. Having said that, some recent stories in the media claim the need for a Master's degree is no longer so critical, so watch this space.

Once you do have a job, you'll find requests for training and education will be looked upon favourably if you can demonstrate how it will prove your performance, or deepen your understanding of your chosen field. In fact, many professional workplaces will have a training plan mapped out for you depending on your chosen career path.

It's also common for employers to pay for formal Norwegian

lessons, if you show a commitment to your studies. This is especially true when the employee has been headhunted from abroad. It's vital to take this investment seriously. If you are still asking to participate in meetings in English after a year of studies, you may find yourself on the receiving end of a few raised eyebrows. Although companies will offer to cover the cost of such tuition, time-off is less common and therefore you should expect to attend classes at least a couple of evenings per week, or at weekends. If you value your free time or you have a young family, consider taking an intensive course upon arrival instead.

THE WORKING LANGUAGE

Many job-seekers are surprised that Norwegian skills are required for a specific job, when the company's website and all the sales material is in English. That's because even in many international offices, the working language outside of formal meetings tends to be Norwegian.

Regardless of the language requirements for the job, learning Norwegian to fluency is expected. Although your Norwegian colleagues will be comfortable switching to English to include you in some of the informal discussions taking place, much of the finer detail will be lost in translation. This is especially true of the chatter over lunch or at breaks. These are the perfect times to sharpen up those language skills!

Norwegian offices of international companies are more likely to use English as the working language, but it will still be an advantage to learn Norwegian for the reasons I just described. It will also be extremely helpful should the job not work out, and you find yourself back on the market.

JOB SECURITY

Employees in Norway are among the most protected anywhere in the world. It is very difficult for a company to fire an employee, even if they are underperforming. Labour unions have a lot of sway here, and will support their members through a disciplinary process. When you get a job, joining the relevant union is a wise move. Dues can appear high, but there are genuine benefits to membership and dues paid can be included on your annual tax return as a deductible.

Trade union websites generally contain a lot of information about the specific industry, such as the biggest employers and salary guidelines. They are usually only published in Norwegian, although some of the bigger associations will have a few information pages in English.

There are also a couple of trade union federations with individual trade unions as their members, and these can be a good starting point for finding out more information about trade unions for specific industries and jobs.

Useful resources:

- Norwegian Confederation of Trade Unions (LO): https://www.lo.no/
- The Confederation of Unions for Professionals (Unio): https://www.unio.no/
- Confederation of Norwegian Enterprise (NHO): https://www.nho.no/

SOCIAL EVENTS

Most offices will have a social committee, which is responsible for arranging a couple of social events each year. There is an unwritten rule that all employees are expected to attend. Your new colleagues will look upon you with disappointment if you choose not to do so.

The events tend to be the same each year. In the late winter, you can expect a skiing trip or possibly a weekend at a cabin to be arranged. A lack of skiing experience is not an excuse not to attend!

This committee will also be responsible for organising the annual *julebord*, the Christmas party usually held in early-to-mid December each year. In contrast to everyday office life, dress code for the Christmas party is formal and it is the one day of the year where you can guarantee to see your colleagues in full formal dress.

Volunteering for the social committee will instantly impress your Norwegian colleagues, and help you to understand Norwegian culture. Speaking of volunteering...

VOLUNTEERING

Volunteering is an important part of Norwegian society, and most Norwegians are members of at least one sports or social club. This concept applies equally so in the work place. Opting to join the social committee is one way to get involved, but even in meetings volunteers are sometimes sought first rather than picking the best person for the job.

Not everyone has the right to live and work in Norway. Before you can even begin your job search, it's critical to fully understand the immigration laws that apply to you.

As with almost every country on the planet, Norway's immigration laws are complex and there are many grey areas. There are several different categories of residence permit based on the needs of Norway, and different rules apply depending on your country of citizenship. These rules are in a constant state of flux.

I'm going to walk you through the overarching rules and concepts that apply, but I urge you to check the specifics that apply to you. Not only are there many exceptions, things do change every year.

The Norwegian Directorate of Immigration (UDI) has an excellent wizard on its website that walks you through the relevant rules that apply to you and your specific circumstances.

A BIG BENEFIT FOR EUROPEANS

Although Norway is not a member of the European Union (EU), it is a member of the European Economic Area (EEA), and must therefore abide by the EEA agreement. Established in 1994, the EEA governs the free movement of people, goods and services within the European Single Market, which includes the freedom to choose residence in any country within this area.

This means that if you are a citizen of one of the EU/EEA member states, you face a much easier task in moving to Norway than citizens of other countries.

That's good news for residents of Austria, Belgium, Bulgaria, Cyprus, Czech Republic, Denmark, Estonia, Finland, France, Germany, Greece, Hungary, Iceland, Ireland, Italy, Latvia, Liechtenstein, Lithuania, Luxembourg, Malta, Netherlands, Poland, Portugal, Romania, Slovakia, Slovenia, Spain, Sweden, Switzerland, and at the time of writing, the United Kingdom.

WHAT ABOUT BRITAIN?

At the time of writing, the United Kingdom is still an EU member, so the rules remain in place. Any future rights of UK citizens with relation to the EEA freedom of movement rules are still uncertain.

The British Ambassador to Norway told The Local: "Some 70 percent of Norway's trade is with the EU, but the UK is Norway's largest market, and Norway the UK's most important energy supplier. We will need new arrangements with

Norway, but we cannot negotiate these whilst the UK is still a member of the EU".

At an open forum at the British Embassy in early 2018, the people responsible for negotiating the Brexit deal told the audience that they hoped any deal with the EU would also be applied to Norway, but the deal with the EU would have to be done first.

If you are British and interested in moving to Norway, I would urge you to make the move sooner rather than later!

IMMIGRATION FOR EUROPEAN CITIZENS

Citizens of an EU/EEA member state have the right to visit, live, work or study in Norway, but must register in order to stay more than three months. You can register using the EU/EEA right of residence system in one of six categories: Employee, student, family member of an EU/EEA national, person with own funds, employee of foreign business, or as self-employed. Only some of these are relevant to job seekers.

Employee / job seeker: If you find a job in Norway, you must register as an employee, which also entitles you to bring your immediate family to Norway. If you are coming to Norway to look for work, you must register with the Police within three months of your arrival. If you do not get a job within six months, you must leave Norway. If you wish to, you can then start the process again and come back to Norway, but you must register again.

Student: To register in this category you must have been admitted to an accredited higher educational institution or an upper secondary school, have enough money to support yourself and any family members, and hold a European Health Insurance Card or prove you have private medical insurance. Registering as a student entitles you to work part-time and bring your immediate family to Norway, who must also register.

An accredited higher education institution is a University, Specialised University College, or a University College of Applied Sciences. The full list of accredited institutions is available from the Norwegian Agency for Quality Assurance in Education.

Person with own funds: You are entitled to register if you can prove you have enough money to support yourself and any family members accompanying you. This is great for wealthy retired people or those with their own business interests or investments in other countries, but is not so suitable for people looking for work. If you are single, you will need to demonstrate income or savings of 186,968kr per year (approx EUR 19,700) before tax. You must also hold a European Health Insurance Card or have private medical insurance.

Employee of foreign business: You are entitled to register in this category if you are an employee of a company registered in an EU/EEA country, or a self-employed individual, that has a contract with a Norwegian company to carry out an assignment in Norway.

Family member of an EU/EEA national: If you have a family member who has registered as an EU/EEA national in Norway, you can also register. Your family member must be able to support you, but you can also work. The specific definition of what constitutes a family member depends on your circumstances, but spouses, registered partners, and children under the age of 21 are typically covered.

Self-employed: You must plan to engage in long-term business activities in Norway through a sole-proprietorship. However, the rules state that in addition to engaging in business activities, you can also take on other work. If you have skills that are in demand, you could register as self-employed to provide an income while looking for a more permanent job.

Citizens of EU/EEA countries only need to register once, regardless of how long you intend to be living in Norway. You can also switch categories (for example go from a student to being employed) without having to re-register. Essentially, the EEA regulations allow for a EU/EEA citizen to simply notify the Police that you are in Norway in order to live and work here. There is no specific work permit required.

IMMIGRATION FOR EVERYONE ELSE

While the registration process for EU/EEA citizens is straightforward, it is unfortunately anything but for everyone else.

Despite rumours to the contrary, there is no such thing as citizenship by descent in Norway. If you had a Norwegian grandmother or great-grandfather, for example, there is no advantage for you in the immigration process.

Immigration rules for non-EU/EEA citizens are vast, varied and complex, and could easily take up a whole book by themselves. The key concept to understand is that you will

only be given a work permit for a specific job. This generally means you will need a job offer in hand before you
receive permission to move to Norway. This lands a lot of
people in a 'chicken and egg' scenario, whereby Norwegian
employers understandably favour people who already have
a right to live and work in Europe.

Another issue to consider is the lengthy process for issuing a
residence permit to non-EU/EEA citizens. It can take
months, which can put off prospective employers. As we
will discuss later, being physically present in Norway
makes it much easier to obtain the required job offer, so
spouses/partners/children of those already working in
Norway have some advantage, as do students, and those
who travel to Norway in order to search for a job.

Visiting Norway: Citizens of some countries can stay in
Norway and the rest of the Schengen area for up to 90 days
without requiring a visa. These include the United States,
Canada, Mexico, Australia, New Zealand, and many countries in Central and South America. If you are planning a
lengthy visit to look for a job, bear in mind that you may be
required to show proof of funds of 500kr per day (approx
USD $65) for the duration of your intended visit. For the
full 90 days, that would amount to 45,000kr (almost USD
$6,000). You also have to have valid travel insurance and
either a reservation for a hotel or a signed paper by friends
that you are staying with them while in Norway (verified by
the local police with a stamp).

Job seeker: In a similar way to the European system,
there is a way for non-Europeans to come to Norway to look
for work for up to six months, albeit with more restrictions.
Applicants must be from a country with visa-free access to

Norway (the same as in Visiting Norway, above), and the applicant must be defined as a Skilled Worker. The definition for this is below, but basically it means you can come to Norway to look for a job such as an engineer or a teacher, for example, but not for unskilled labour.

The other big restriction is that you must have funds to sustain yourself for the period of job seeking, and you are not allowed to work in Norway during that time. You must have at least 20,248kr per month (approx USD $2,500), or a total of 121,483kr (approx. USD $14,800) for the full six month period. If you come to Norway as a skilled job seeker and are unsuccessful, you must wait one full year before applying again.

To obtain a work permit, you must apply in one of the following categories: Skilled workers, seasonal workers, vocational training and research, diplomats and NATO personnel, seafarers, and employees of foreign companies in another EU/EEA country.

Skilled workers: If you have completed higher education or have completed vocational training, you can apply for a residence permit as a skilled worker. You must normally already have received a job offer, or have your own business.

Skilled workers with a job offer from a Norwegian employer must have completed a vocational training programme of at least three years, completed a bachelor's degree, or prove special qualifications through long experience, although the latter is only granted in exceptional cases. You must be paid at least the standard wage where a collective agreement applies. If there is no collective agreement for the industry, your pre-tax annual salary must be at least 421,700kr if the job requires a master's degree, or at least 391,800kr if the job requires a bachelor's degree. In this category of permit, you can normally bring your close family with you.

Job seekers can apply for this permit for up to six months, but they must fall into the skilled worker category as defined above.

Employee of international company: You must apply for this type of permit if you are employed by an international company and are going to carry out an assignment for the Norwegian branch of the international company. There is also a permit if you are employed by a company abroad that has a contract with an enterprise in Norway to carry out an assignment in Norway. Professional qualification and wage requirements are similar to the skilled worker category.

Offshore workers: In order to work offshore in the Norwegian oil & gas industry you need this permit. Some exceptions apply.

Athletes or coaches: You must either be an athlete who is going to participate in top-level sports or a coach in top-level sports. Examples include the top two divisions in men's football and the top division in ice hockey. The pay must be at least 242,966kr per year pre-tax and the Department of Immigration will consider each application on an individual basis.

Ethnic cook: You must have received a concrete offer of full-time employment from one specific employer in Norway. You cannot work at several restaurants, even if they have the same owner. You must have at least ten years' relevant education and/or work experience and must have worked at a high-standard hotel/restaurant for at least half of that period. If you are from China, you must have a certificate from the authorities stating that you are a 'level 1' cook or a 'level 2' cook.

If you are from Thailand, you must have a certificate from the authorities stating that you are a 'level 2' cook. You will in principle only be granted a residence permit as an ethnic cook in exceptional circumstances.

Religious leaders / teachers: In principle, you must have a master's degree in your religion or in pedagogics from a university/ university college. You must have received a concrete offer of full-time employment from one specific employer in Norway and the pay and working conditions must not be poorer than is normal in Norway, except in certain circumstances.

Self-employment: It is possible to move to Norway with the intent of working on a self-employed basis, but this is not straightforward. The business you are intending to run must be directly related to your professional education, and you must be expecting to earn at least 242,966kr per year pre-tax. Another downside is that this permit is only granted for one-year at a time, and so must be renewed every year. If you don't make the income requirement, your application will likely be rejected.

Study permit: If you wish to study or go to school in Norway for more than three months, you must apply for a study permit. If you are granted a study permit, you will also be able to work for up to 20 hours a week while you are studying and full-time during holidays. To gain this permit, you must have received an offer of admission to a full-time study programme at a university college or university, and you must have at least 116,369kr per year in documented wealth or income to live on.

Au pair: As an au pair, you can improve your language skills and learn about Norwegian society by living with a Norwegian family. In return, you will provide services such as light housework and/or child care for the host family.

You must be between the ages of 18 and 30, and cannot have any children of your own. It must be likely that you will return to your home country at the end of your stay in Norway, and the circumstances in your home country must also indicate that you can return.

Useful resources:

- Norwegian Directorate of Immigration: https://www.udi.no/
- Norwegian Agency for Quality Assurance in Education: http://www.nokut.no/en/

Generally speaking, working conditions in Norway are among the best in the world. Legislation and labour laws fall heavily on the side of the employee. Once you've got a job, you are protected in many ways and it is difficult for a company to fire you.

Depending on your status in Norway, if you lose your job then the Norwegian government steps in to provide a generous welfare benefit and various programs to get you back into work. We already looked at the working hours and vacation allowance in the working culture chapter, so let's now take a closer look at salaries.

SALARIES IN NORWAY

Salaries in Norway are much higher than in many European countries. This is especially true at the lower end of the labour market, such as for cleaners, restaurant workers and manual labourers. However, at the higher end such as for senior management, salaries can often not be as competitive as some other countries.

Contrary to popular belief, there is no national minimum wage written into Norwegian law. Despite this, almost everyone receives a fair living wage. Why? Because Norway is heavily unionised and the vast majority of employees belong to a trade union. These unions come to collective agreements on salaries and working conditions with companies, which are then applied to all workers, not just union members. This general application of the collective agreements is in place partly to help prevent foreign workers from being taken advantage of.

Generally speaking, collective agreements feature one fixed hourly rate for everyone over the age of 18. There are often different rates to distinguish skilled from unskilled work, for overtime, and for younger workers.

For example, in the construction industry, skilled workers earn a minimum of 197.90kr per hour, while unskilled workers with no experience earn at least 177.80kr per hour. That rises to 185.50kr after one year's experience. Young workers under the age of 18 must earn at least 119.30kr.

People employed as cleaners must earn a minimum of 177.63kr if they are over 18, and 129.59kr if not. There is also a guaranteed pay supplement of at least 26kr per hour for work between 9pm and 6am, which is agreed on an individual basis.

For those employed in hotels, restaurants and catering, workers over 20 years of age and those 18 years old and above with at least four months of work experience must earn at least 157.18kr per hour. There are lower rates for younger workers.

In industries where there is no collective agreement, there are published standards for most jobs so with some research (in Norwegian, of course) on the websites of industry associations, you will know what to expect.

Useful resources:

- Minimum Wage in Norway: https://www.lifeinnorway.net/norway-minimum-wage/

HOLIDAY PAY

I wrote earlier about the generous amount of holiday days given in Norway. However, holiday pay is a different thing, and this is something that trips up many newcomers.

I remember how confusing and frustrating the system was during my first year here, but now it just makes sense and seems normal.

While the exact implementation of the rules does vary between companies, in general holiday pay is accrued the year before holidays are taken, and then paid instead of ordinary pay during holiday absence.

This means that although employees who did not work the previous year are entitled to take holidays, they are not entitled to holiday pay. So in your first year working in Norway, be sure to save enough to cover this drop in income, and check with your HR representative to understand exactly how your payroll system works with holiday pay.

On the plus side, whenever you leave a job the outstanding amount of holiday pay is paid to you with your final payslip. When I left my job to start a business, this was a really useful sum to have in the bank.

Many people moving to Norway from large countries such as the UK or USA are surprised at the lack of opportunities available in some sectors.

The reason is actually pretty simple. Norway is a relatively small country - a population of under six million - with a unique economy. Some sectors are much bigger than in other countries, while others are almost non-existent.

This isn't intended as an exhaustive guide into every industry in Norway, but rather to introduce the biggest and most important sectors to consider when it comes to finding work as a newcomer. It should serve as useful background information for your job search.

OIL AND GAS

The oil and gas industry remains Norway's most important, accounting for approximately 14% of GDP and an astonishing 39% of total exports. There's even a petroleum museum in Stavanger, which is well worth a visit if you're ever in the area!

Norway's biggest industry is in a phase of recovery following the widely-reported oil price slump, and employment opportunities are beginning to return. From 2013 to 2016, it's estimated that almost 50,000 oil and gas jobs in Norway were lost. That's a massive number considering the country's population of little more than five million. The impact was felt hardest in cities like Stavanger and particularly among international workers.

Although employee numbers are unlikely to return to the highs of ten years ago, the early signs point towards Norway's major energy companies hiring more employees in the years to come. Equnior's USD $6bn Johan Castberg oilfield will become the northernmost development on the Norwegian Continental Shelf, while Aker BP has submitted plans for three projects worth a total of USD $1.9bn

Qualified international employees are commonplace in both offshore and onshore jobs. Many of the companies operating on the Norwegian Continental Shelf are global and bring in employees from all over the world to work on a project basis. Salaries are high, but the work can be tough.

Useful resources:

- Norwegian Petroleum:
  https://www.norskpetroleum.no/en/
- Norwegian Oil & Gas Association:
  https://www.norskoljeoggass.no/en/

SEAFOOD

The cold waters off Norway's lengthy coastline are famous for their oil and gas, but just as important to the Norwegian economy is the seafood. After the oil and gas industry, fisheries and aquaculture is Norway's largest export industry with products from captured and farmed fish exported to more than 150 countries around the world.

A good place to start your research is the Norwegian Seafood Federation (formerly known as FHL), which represents the interests of around 550 member companies. According to the federation, 38 million meals of Norwegian seafood are served worldwide, every single day of the year.

Useful resources:

- Norwegian Seafood Federation: https://sjomatnorge.no/norwegian-seafood-federation/
- Norwegian Seafood Association: http://www.nsl.no/english

MARITIME

Shipping has long been a hugely important industry for Norway, but it is set to take centre stage as oil and gas becomes increasingly harder and more expensive to drill.

Internationally, Norway is known for its forward-thinking maritime policy and research & development teams, all working towards helping the shipping industry meet the challenging future goals of the Paris Climate Agreement.

Of the first 50 LNG-propelled ships, all but five were Norwegian. The world's first battery-powered electric car ferry entered service on the Sognefjord in 2015, and that development is set to continue. The government has announced that by 2026, only zero-emission ferries will be allowed on its fjords.

Jobs in the maritime industry range from engineering positions with large multinationals through to research and development work with small startups working on some of the next-generation technologies.

Useful resources:

- Blue Maritime Cluster:
  http://www.bluemaritimecluster.no/gce
- Maritime Clean Tech:
  https://maritimecleantech.no
- Norwegian Shipowners Association:
  https://www.rederi.no/en

INFORMATION AND COMMUNICATIONS TECHNOLOGY (ICT)

According to government figures, around 80,000 people work in Norway's ICT industry. That's a number that's rapidly growing as the industry becomes of increasingly importance to the country's economy.

The bulk of the country's ICT industry is telecommunications, and much of that is spearheaded by Telenor. Outside telecoms, the industry includes everything from data operations, IT services and software producers, through to consultancy services.

While not as renowned on the world stage as Stockholm or Helsinki, the Oslo startup scene is attracting attention and investment from around the world. This means there are a whole host of small startup companies that are looking for talent, and many are happy to consider English speakers.

Useful resources:

- ICT Norway: https://www.ikt-norge.no/english/
- Startup Norway: http://www.startupnorway.com
- Electrician and IT workers union: https://elogit.no/

RESEARCH

The academic field is one of the top areas of employment for international workers. Norway's public universities hire experts in all research areas, but there is a focus on energy, ocean sciences and ICT. Salaries are better than in many countries but that has to be balanced with an increased cost of living. Depending on the institute, role and candidate, a postdoctoral position tends to carry an annual salary of around 450,000kr, while research scientists should earn at least 500,000kr. Competition for positions is high.

Research is one of the few areas in which fluency in the language is not required, but it is preferred and researchers in long-term positions will be expected to learn Norwegian.

Many of the opportunities are funded directly or indirectly by the Research Council of Norway (Forskningsrådet), which operates large-scale funding programmes in key research areas. This is a good place to start your investigations into working in Norwegian research.

Many jobs are offered through personal contacts, even if they have been or are planned to be advertised. Personal networking is critical within research and people within these academic networks are often approached directly about open positions, even when vacancies have to be advertised externally. So the best advice I can give you is to build your own academic network and make connections with relevant researchers already working in Norway.

Useful resources:

- Norwegian Association of Researchers:
  https://www.forskerforbundet.no/english/
- Norwegian Society of Graduate Technical and Scientific Professionals (Tekna):
  https://www.tekna.no/en

TOURISM & HOSPITALITY

Norway's tourism industry is booming, but work tends to be seasonal so the opportunities for full-time employment are not as strong as you might expect. Many tourist attractions hire temporary staff for the June to August period, with January-April employment opportunities common in winter sport resorts. While seasonal work might not be what you're looking for, it could be an ideal way to getting some valuable Norwegian work experience onto your CV/resume.

Another common area in which foreigners are employed is the hotel and hospitality industry. They are among the few jobs in Norway where Norwegian is not necessarily required, but the work is seasonal and the pay can be very low. Many new immigrants to Norway can get jobs as cleaners, in housekeeping, or in the kitchens at Norwegian hotels.

Although fluent Norwegian isn't required to get started, you will need language skills to progress beyond basic work and for client-facing roles such as reception work. In most tourism and hospitality jobs, your chances of landing a position will increase if you can speak other languages. Fluent German is particularly sought after, but Spanish and Italian can be useful too.

Tourism is increasing fast from Asian countries, so those with skills in Chinese, Japanese and Korean languages are likely to be in high demand in the years to come.

CONSTRUCTION

The country's infrastructure is under constant improvement, with new roads, bridges, tunnels, rail lines, schools, hospitals and housing all under construction at the time of writing. According to industry figures, an additional 10,000 construction workers will be needed every year in Norway until 2020. Having said that, the sector is extremely sensitive to market pressures and fluctuations, and is often the industry that first feels the signs of economic change.

A large number of public sector projects drive the industry, and unlike in many other countries, the Norwegian sector consists of many small companies. Around 200,000 people work in the industry in a total of 50,000 companies, many of which are single-person businesses.

Qualified labour in manual trades can be hard to find among Norway's small population, so many firms look to foreigners for the required skills. Typically, these jobs go to citizens from EU countries who are much easier for Norwegian companies to hire.

Useful resources:

- Norwegian Contractors Association: http://www.eba.no/
- The Federation of Norwegian Construction Industries: http://www.eba.no/
- Industry magazine: http://www.bygg.no/

HEALTHCARE

As a relatively small country, Norway has a shortage of qualified professionals in some industries. Healthcare is one of those. As the country's population continues to grow and people live ever longer lives, this need looks set to grow

The most common employers of nurses are hospitals, and health and care services provided by local authorities. These include care homes, nursing homes, in-home nursing, health services in schools, and public health centres.

Norwegian healthcare is administered by four regional authorities covering the south-east, west, central and northern regions. Each authority is responsible for its region's hospitals and the employment of healthcare professionals. Local authorities take responsibility for care of the elderly and other care services.

Foreign nurses are welcome to apply for authorisation to work as a nurse in Norway, but the biggest stumbling block is that your education must equal Norwegian standards. Almost all healthcare employers in Norway require their staff – doctors, psychologists, nurses, physiotherapists, phar-macologists, bioengineers, auxiliary nurses and care assis-tants – to have formal authorisation from the Directorate for Health and Social Affairs. You can apply for authorisation, which gives you full rights to practise your profession, or apply for a licence to work for a period until you acquire full authorisation.

The number one requirement to work as a nurse in Norway is a degree in general nursing. To be considered for authori-sation, EU/EEA citizens must have qualifications that entitle them to work in their home country. Since January 2017, applicants with education from outside the EU/EEA are subject to additional language requirements. Speaking Norwegian at a relatively advanced level is now a prerequi-site. Be warned that the waiting list for authorisation is long, especially for citizens of countries from outside the EU/EEA.

Useful resources:

Norwegian Nurses Association: https://www.nsf.no/

Authorisation and License for Health Personnel: https://helsedirektoratet.no/English

AU PAIRS / NANNYS

While these aren't long-term careers, working as an au pair offers a taste of Norwegian culture and lifestyle, and the chance to improve your language skills. In return for accom-modation, meals and a small income, you will provide child-care and do light housework for the host family.

While employment law applies to au pairs and you are entitled to a salary and holiday pay, do your research first. According to the Norwegian Union of Municipal and General Employees, there are around 3,000 au pairs working in Norway at any given time. Most of the au pairs are from the Philippines and are in their 20s.

Work opportunities will vary wildly depending on your personal circumstances and experience. This section is designed to introduce you to some of the biggest employers in Norway, in the public sector, academic world, and private companies.

PUBLIC SECTOR

By far the biggest employer in Norway is the public sector. According to data from Statistics Norway, around 170,000 people are employed by central government, more than 500,000 people are employed by local municipalities, and a further 50,000 are employed at regional level. That's a total of almost three-quarters of a million people, in a country with a total population of just over five million.

Following the Second World War, successive Norwegian governments sought to broaden and extend public benefits to its citizens through sickness and disability benefits, guaranteed pensions, heavily subsidised universal healthcare, and unemployment benefits. Infrastructure spending has also been relatively high over the last few decades, with projects such as new hospitals, schools, housing estates, roads, railway lines, bridges and underwater tunnels having been completed or underway across the country.

In recent years, an increased focus on the digitalisation of public services has changed the mix of job opportunities available across the public sector.

It should go without saying that all public-facing jobs will require an advanced level of Norwegian. However, a lot of public sector work is put out to contract and done by private companies. There may be opportunities here for foreigners, especially in the areas of ICT.

THE ACADEMIC WORLD

Norway's universities and research institutes are a major employer of international talent. Working in this environment can be rewarding, but competition for vacancies is tough. PhD research positions are especially competitive given the relatively high salaries on offer compared to many other countries.

The biggest areas of research in Norway are in energy (both fossil-fuels and renewables), ocean sciences and ICT. These are key areas for the development of the future Norwegian economy and as such, international talent is sought-after. Research is one of the few areas in which fluency in the language is not required, but it is preferred and researchers in long-term positions will be expected to learn Norwegian.

Listed below are some of the main universities and research institutes in Norway, along with their specialisms. It's also worth registering with EURES, which is the European job mobility portal. While not specific to Norway or to research jobs, many do get listed there.

University of Oslo: Interdisciplinary strategic research areas include life sciences, energy, the Nordic countries, the Arctic, global governance, and religion in pluralist societies. 25 percent of the academic staff and 31 percent of PhD candidates are non-Norwegians.

- Website: http://www.uio.no/english/
- Careers information: http://www.uio.no/english/about/jobs/vacancies/

University of Bergen: Strategic research areas at the University of Bergen include marine research, global social challenges, and climate and energy transition. Norwegian Centres of Excellence (SFF) based at the University include geobiology, intervention science in maternal and child health, early sapiens behaviour, space science, and cancer biomarkers.

- Website: http://www.uib.no/en
- Careers information: http://www.uib.no/en/about/84777/vacant-positions-uib

University of Stavanger: Research at the University of Stavanger is organised into six faculties: Arts and education, health sciences, performing arts, science and technology (including a significant focus on engineering), social sciences, and business. The University is also home to the International Research Institute of Stavanger, the Centre for learning environment and behavioural research, and the Reading Centre.

- Website: http://www.uis.no/
- Careers information: http://www.uis.no/job-opportunities/vacant-positions/

Norwegian University of Science and Technology (NTNU): The Trondheim-based NTNU has recently expanded to include campuses in Ålesund and Gjøvik. Strategic research areas include energy, health, oceans and sustainability. Research centres hosted by NTNU include Cyber and Information Security, Health Promotion Research, Digital Life Norway, The Hunt Study (a longitudinal population health study), and the K.G. Jebsen Centres for exercise in medicine, genetic epidemiology, and myeloma research.

- Website: http://www.ntnu.edu
- Careers information:
  https://www.ntnu.edu/vacancies

SINTEF: SINTEF is the largest independent research organisation in Scandinavia with more than 2,000 employees of 75 nationalities, most which work in Trondheim and Oslo. SINTEF is a broad, multidisciplinary research institute with expertise in renewable energy, ocean, building and infrastructure, digitalization, climate and environment, industry, society, microtechnology and nanotechnology, oil and gas, health and welfare, materials, and biotechnology.

- Website: http://www.sintef.no/
- Careers information:
  http://www.sintef.no/en/sintef-is-looking-for-the-
  next-generation-of-probl/vacant-positions/

Norwegian University of Life Sciences (NMBU):
Based south of Oslo in Ås, NMBU conducts
interdisciplinary research to generate innovations in food,
health, environmental protection, climate and the sustainable use of natural resources. Around 1,700 employees
work here.

- Website: https://www.nmbu.no/
- Careers information:
  https://www.nmbu.no/en/about-nmbu/positions

Norwegian Business School (BI): The private business school BI has campuses in all four of Norway's biggest
cities: Oslo, Bergen, Stavanger, and Trondheim. Research
centres include multisensory marketing, corporate governance research, creative industries, health care management, applied macro- and petroleum economics, and more.

- Website: https://www.bi.edu
- Careers information: https://www.bi.edu/about-
  bi/vacant-positions/

There are many other smaller universities, colleges and
academic institutions that hire staff. If your expertise lies in
this area, you can get the full list of institutions at
https://www.lifeinnorway.net/study-in-norway/

THE PRIVATE SECTOR

These are the biggest companies as defined by leading Norwegian business magazine Kapital (kapital.no). They are not necessarily the biggest employers, but many on this list do employ thousands of people.

There has been a trend in recent years that unscrupulous individuals are promising job opportunities on behalf of some of Norway's biggest companies. They ask for payments to cover processing fees, visas, work permits and so on, which never materialise. No Norwegian company will require you to make advance payments as part of the hiring process.

"Be patient and look for international workplaces if possible. International companies are more likely to see the value in finding talent from other cultures and international markets, and expats will likely find that it makes for a more dynamic and accepting workplace." - Liz Bondelid

---

Equinor: Still better known by their former name of Statoil, Equinor is an international energy company and the world's largest offshore operator, with more than 20,500 employees and operations in over 30 countries worldwide. The company operates 42 fields and platforms in Norway, and employs 18,977 people. Many are based at their Oslo headquarters or in Stavanger.

- Company website: https://www.equnior.com

- Careers information:
  https://www.equinor.com/en/careers.html

Telenor: Telenor is a leading global telecommunications company with a leading position in mobile, broadband and TV services in the Nordic region. They operate in 13 countries with 33,000 employees worldwide. Many of the employees in Norway work from the Oslo headquarters, but there is also a wide network of retail stores across the country.

- Company website: https://www.telenor.com
- Careers information:
  https://www.telenor.com/career/

Yara International: Chemical company Yara delivers profitable and responsible solutions for agriculture and the environment. Its largest business area is the production of nitrogen fertilizer, with further interests in nitrates, ammonia, urea and other nitrogen-based chemicals. The Norwegian government is the largest shareholder, owning more than one-third of the company. Approximately 12,500 employees work for Yara across the world, with much of the research and development work taking place in Norway.

- Company website: http://yara.com
- Careers information: http://yara.com/careers/

Norsk Hydro: Known by most simply as Hydro, the company is a global supplier of aluminium. Hydro runs many aluminium processing facilities throughout Norway, including many in rural areas such as Sunndal in Møre og Romsdal county. In October 2017, Hydro completed the takeover of Sapa, a global leader in extruded aluminium solutions, to create an even bigger force in the industry.

- Company website: https://www.hydro.com
- Careers information: https://www.hydro.com/en/careers/

NorgesGruppen: Traditionally the largest player in Norwegian food retail, NorgesGruppen is a major whole-saling group and owner of the retail supermarket chains Kiwi, Meny, Joker and Spar. More than 28,000 people work in the various businesses owned by the group, with a further 10,000 employed in franchised operations, making Norges-Gruppen one of Norway's biggest employers.

- Company website: http://www.norgesgruppen.no
- Careers information: http://www.norgesgruppen.no/muligheter/ledige-stillinger/

DNB: DNB is Norway's largest financial services group and one of the largest in the Nordic region in terms of market capitalisation. The group offers a full range of finan-cial services, including loans, savings, advisory services, insurance and pension products for both personal and corporate customers.

- Company website: https://www.dnb.no/
- Careers information: https://www.dnb.no/en/about-us/careers.html

KLP: Kommunal Landspensjonskasse (KLP) is Norway's largest life insurance company, delivering financial and insurance services to the public sector and its employees. The company and its subsidiaries employ almost 1,000 people in Norway.

- Company website: https://www.klp.no/
- Careers information: http://english.klp.no/about-klp/working-at-klp

Reitangruppen: The Trondheim-based retail giant Reitangruppen employs around 38,000 people across Scandinavia and the Baltic countries. Its main retail brands include the Rema 1000 supermarket chain and the Uno-X Energy service stations, but they also have significant real estate and investment interests.

- Company website: http://www.reitangruppen.no
- Careers information: http://www.reitangruppen.no/a-arbeide-i-reitangruppen/

Storebrand: Norway's largest asset manager and one of the leading players in the Nordics, Storebrand manages more than 570 billion kroner in long-term savings and insurance. The company has provided occupational pensions to Norwegian employees since 1917, which is a full 50 years before social security was established. They are headquartered in Lysaker, Oslo.

- Company website: https://www.storebrand.no
- Careers information:

https://www.storebrand.no/om-storebrand/jobb-
og-karriere

Statkraft: Statkraft is a leading global company in hydropower and Europe's largest generator of renewable energy. The group produces hydropower, wind power, solar power, gas-fired power, and also supplies district heating solutions in many Norwegian towns. Statkraft has 3,800 employees in 16 countries, and is headquartered in Lilleaker, Oslo.

- Company website: https://www.statkraft.com
- Careers information:
  https://www.statkraft.com/career/

Coop Norge: Coop Norge is a Norwegian cooperative owned by 117 local cooperatives with more than 1.3 million members. Their retail brands include Obs, Coop Prix, Coop Mega, Matkroken, Obs Bygg, and Extra. The group employs around 18,000 people in their retail stores, logistics and other administrative functions.

- Company website: https://coop.no
- Careers information: https://coop.no/om-
  coop/ledige-stillinger/

ExxonMobil Norge: With a history of more than 120 years operating in Norway, ExxonMobil is one of the largest oil and gas producers on the Norwegian Continental Shelf. In addition, the company has ownership interests in more than 20 producing fields operated by Equinor and Shell. Operational activities are conducted from their Stavanger headquarters, commercial functions take place in Skøyen, Oslo, and their refinery is located in Tønsberg. The company also owns and operates 250 Esso and Mobil branded service stations across the country.

- Company website: http://www.exxonmobil.no
- Careers information: http://www.exxonmobil.no/nn-no/company/careers/careers-in-norway/

Orkla: Orkla is a leading supplier of branded consumer goods to the grocery, out-of home, specialised retail, pharmacy and bakery sectors in the Nordics, Baltics and central Europe. The Orkla group also holds strong positions in selected product categories in India. Headquartered in Oslo, the group employs more than 18,000 people.

- Company website: http://www.orkla.no
- Careers information: http://www.orkla.no/Karriere

Marine Harvest Norway: Norway's largest aquaculture company employs more than 1,600 employees. They cover the entire value chain from feed production through to processing and distribution. Most of the salmon from their operations in Norway is exported to Europe, the United States and Asia. The global headquarters are in Bergen.

- Company website: http://marineharvest.no
- Careers information: http://marineharvest.no/mennesker/

Norsk Tipping: Norsk Tipping is a government-owned company under the direction of the Ministry of Culture. They operate a variety of lottery games, instant-win games and a sports bookmaker in a highly-regulated marketplace. Approximately 12 million Norwegian kroner per day is generated for good causes by the company, which employs more than 400 people mainly at their headquarters in Hamar.

- Company website: https://www.norsk-tipping.no
- Careers information: https://www.norsk-tipping.no/selskapet/karriere

Atea: As northern Europe's leading IT infrastructure company, Atea's 4,000 consultants help a wide range of customers design, implement and operate complex IT solutions from multiple vendors. Although headquartered in eastern Oslo, Atea has a presence in all parts of Norway and consultants often work on customer sites.

- Company website: https://www.atea.com
- Careers information: https://www.atea.no/karriere/

Subsea 7 Norway: Subsea 7 is a world-leading seabed-to-surface engineering, construction and services contractor to the offshore energy industry. They provide engineering and construction solutions to complex projects in all water depths and challenging environments. The company also owns EMAS Chiyoda Subsea (ECS), i-Tech Services, Seaway Heavy Lifting, and Swagelining Limited.

- Company website: https://www.subsea7.com/

- Careers information:
  https://www.subsea7.com/en/our-
  people/working-for-subsea7.html

Veidekke: One of Scandinavia's largest contractors and property developers, Veidekke carries out all types of construction projects, from residential developments to maintaining roads. Half of the 7,400 employees own shares in the company. Veidekke is headquartered in Oslo but jobs are available in all parts of the country.

- Company website: http://veidekke.no
- Careers information: http://veidekke.no/jobb/

Gjensidige Forsikring: Gjensidige is a leading Nordic insurance group listed on the Oslo Stock Exchange. Gjensidige has provided insurance services for 200 years, and its 4,000 employees work to offer products in Norway, Denmark Sweden and the Baltic States. In Norway, the company also offers banking, pensions and savings accounts. Most of the jobs in Norway are based at their Oslo headquarters.

- Company website: https://www.gjensidige.no
- Careers information:
  https://www.gjensidige.no/konsern/jobb

Seadrill: Seadrill is a leading global offshore drilling contractor with operations in Dubai, Houston, Rio de Janeiro and Ciudad del Carmen along with Oslo. Seadrill and its affiliates own or lease 51 drilling rigs. The majority of the company's employees work offshore, but there are also a variety of onshore operational support roles in both engineering and non-engineering functions.

- Company website: http://www.seadrill.com
- Careers information: http://www.seadrillcareers.com

MøllerGruppen: One of northern Europe's leading automotive groups, MøllerGruppen's core operations involve the import, sales and service of Volkswagen, Audi and Skoda cars to Norway, Sweden, Estonia, Lithuania and Latvia. The group also has significant real estate interests.

- Company website: http://www.moller.no/
- Careers information: http://www.moller.no/en/About/Career-opportunities/Norway/

Norwegian Air Shuttle: Norwegian is the sixth largest low-cost carrier in the world with around 7,000 employees. Although known internationally for their low-cost long-haul model, Norwegian remains an important domestic carrier in Norway. The airline operates one of the newest and greenest fleets of airplanes in Europe. Career opportunities include pilots, cabin crew, engineering and maintenance, and a variety of support roles.

- Company website: https://www.norwegian.com/
- Careers information: http://careers.norwegian.com/

Aker Solutions: Aker Solutions is a global provider of

products, systems and services to the oil and gas industry. Its engineering, design and technology teams work on all manner of projects from shallow to ultra-deep waters and tropical to arctic conditions, often in collaboration with other companies. The company employs around 14,000 employees worldwide.

- Company website: http://akersolutions.com
- Careers information: http://akersolutions.com/careers/

Posten: With a staff approaching 18,000, the Norwegian postal service is a major employer through their brands Posten and Bring. In addition to jobs delivering mail and working in post office branches, the number of employees working in ICT on digital solutions is increasing.

- Company website: https://www.postennorge.no
- Careers information: https://www.postennorge.no/jobb

Total E&P Norge: The Norwegian branch of the global oil and gas giant explores for and produces oil and gas on the Norwegian Continental Shelf. It holds exploration licenses in the North Sea, the Norwegian Sea, and the Barents Sea.

- Company website: http://www.total.no/en
- Careers information: http://www.total.no/en/better-energy-you

Wilh. Wilhemsen: A global maritime industry group and

industry leader headquartered in Oslo. The Wilhelmsen group includes a variety of shipping and logistics companies, which offer employment opportunities in everything from engineering and seafaring to logistics planning.

- Company website: https://www.wilhelmsen.com
- Careers information:
  https://www.wilhelmsen.com/careers/

Other notable companies in the top 50 not listed above include Tine Gruppen (dairy products), Norske Shell (oil and gas), DNV GL (quality assurance and risk management), Nordea (banking), Schibsted (media), Kongsberg Gruppen (engineering technology), Ferd Holding (investment company), ConocoPhillips Norge (oil and gas), NSB (state railway), and Hafslund (power).

SMALL EMPLOYERS

Norway's startup scene is small compared to our neighbours in Sweden, Denmark and Finland, but it is growing fast. Five years ago there were no coworking or entrepreneurial spaces in Trondheim, whereas today there are at least four. A lot of public money has gone into stimulating such an environment where ideas can be turned into businesses, and even private companies are starting to support the creation of new businesses.

But there is a big difference between the world of technology startups chasing investment, and sustainable small businesses that employ several people and consistently turn a profit. Norway has a lot of the latter, everything from small independent shops and cafes through to advertising agencies and consulting firms - and everything in between.

There's a lot of benefits to working for a small employer. Salaries will often be lower, but the flexibility, varied tasks and job prospects as the company grows can easily outweigh that. You may also find that small employers are more open to hiring someone with no or basic Norwegian skills, but only if the work is language independent. For instance, a graphic design agency or architecture firm may well hire non-Norwegian speakers, but an advertising agency probably won't, unless they only work with international clients.

The biggest problem you'll face is identifying small employers that are looking to hire. Including a list of 'biggest small employers' in this book naturally makes little sense. If you're interested in working for a startup or a small company, you'll have to do some research.

Realistically, this means being physically in Norway is a requirement to stand a chance of securing a job with any small company. If you are not yet in Norway, you can make a start by building up a professional and personal network in your target city. We'll talk a lot more about this process in the chapter on looking for a job in person.

Useful Resources:

• Startup Norway: http://www.startupnorway.com/

INGRID

To start out, I would like to say that job seeking is not an exact science.

There is no secret formula to follow in order to guarantee success, but there are many things you can do to increase your chances.

You have to find the right mix of ingredients: learning how to sell yourself, creating a professional network, taking initiative, not giving up, and last but not least; for the right opportunity to present itself at the right time.

I will show you how the social structure of work life in Norway is built up, so that you are better equipped to navigate yourself as a job seeker here. Since job seeking is first and foremost about people and sales, and secondly about what is written on your CV and application, it is important that you know the social codes of how to find a job in Norway.

Of course, social codes are never completely rigid. Everyone is different, and someone who is good at reading social settings can bend social rules to their benefit. Keep that in mind when reading this book. Take the advice and try it out, but maybe once you have truly understood Norwegian society and social norms, you will find your own way that works better for you.

My advice is based on several years of my own experience being a job seeker in Norway, and then, just as importantly, years of helping foreign job seekers just like you find a job in Norway.

Many job seekers I talk to say something like, "Oh yeah, of course you know all the ins and outs of job seeking in Norway because you are a Norwegian!"

But that's not really what matters. My advice is good advice because of my experience spending time with foreign job seekers on their journey to a new career. I've heard their stories, I've seen their mistakes, and I've helped them through it all.

I've seen it so many times, and I have been jumping for joy so many times when one of my job seekers finds a job, that I can tell you for sure what works and what does not work. The majority of successful job seekers I have met have been on a similar journey.

They start out by just sitting at home applying to open positions online, and nothing happens. Once the light bulb turns on and they understand the personal aspect of job seeking in Norway, they become more proactive by networking and showing up in-person. Soon, they start to see results and eventually find a job.

As I said at the beginning of this chapter, finding a job is not an exact science and there is no one guaranteed way to succeed. You need to try various avenues and find the one that works for you and your circumstances. To illustrate this point, take a look at these results from the Life in Norway survey.

Life in Norway Survey: How did you first learn about your job?

16.7%: A friend or colleague

16.7%: The Finn.no website

11.1%: Networking in person

8.3%: NAV (Norwegian Labour and Welfare Administration)

8.3%: Networking online

5.6%: LinkedIn

33.3%: Others, including: jobs page on lifeinnorway.net, recruitment company, newspaper advert, LinkedIn, headhunter, other job websites.

TIMING IS EVERYTHING

When it comes to applying for jobs in Norway, it is important to keep in mind the calendar. There are some times of the year when very few jobs are advertised. I would go as far as to say that looking for work during July and December can in many cases be pointless.

During July, most companies have what is called *fellesferie*, which basically means that there are three weeks where the employer can ask their employees to take summer vacation. In mid-July, the streets of Oslo can be deserted and the only people you'll see are almost certainly foreign tourists.

During these months, your time would be better spent working on your Norwegian language skills, or even simply enjoying your own summer vacation. Some stress-free weeks could be just what you need to recharge the batteries before things start to ramp up again at the beginning of August.

In December, people are more worried about plans for the Christmas holiday and work Christmas party than hiring new staff. With budgets closing for the year, positions are few and far between. Do keep an eye out for relevant positions, but do not expect too much to happen until at least the second week of the new year.

When it comes to time management, I suggest not waiting when you see a position that interests you. In some cases, applications and job interviews are handled as they are sent in. Not all employers wait for the deadline to review applications, as is customary in some countries.

This is especially true for recruitment agencies as they are frequently hiring replacements needed because of extended sick leave or maternity leave. In these cases, time is of the essence.

Applying quickly should be an important part of your strategy to stand out. It is much easier to get noticed if the person reading your application hasn't already gone through fifty others.

YOUR ATTITUDE

I would like to say something to you, very honestly: as a job seeker you have my deepest empathy.

Looking for a job is really, really hard work, both in terms of the hours you have to put in before finding the right job, and in the physiological stress that comes with it.

You are basically selling your professional self, and for each time you send in a job application, for each time you go to a networking event, or show up unannounced at a company you would like to work for, you are putting yourself out there for evaluation.

Each time the answer is no, your confidence takes a hit. It takes a very strong person indeed to avoid feeling as if you yourself are being rejected. I always tell job seekers to avoid taking it personally, because 99 percent of the time the reason they did not choose you is something outside of your control.

For example, maybe the company have many female employees and prefer to hire a man to balance out the work environment, and you happen to be a woman. Perhaps they are looking for a specific skill or experience that they neglected to include on the job advertisement.

However, I know not taking these things personally is much easier said than done. I know it, because I have been in your shoes. That is why I want to tell you to give yourself credit, perhaps even treat yourself with a slice of cake or an ice-cream, every time you put yourself out there and do something you find scary.

When you have to face a rejection, remember to give yourself some time before getting back in the saddle. Do something else to take your mind of things – go out with friends or enjoy the voluntary work you are doing. Whatever you choose to do, avoid staying in a state of self-pity for too long, since your level of success as a job seeker equals the amount of effort and positive attitude that you put in. No one will knock on your door telling you that they have a job offer for you. This is all up to you and how much initiative you take, and that starts with a positive attitude.

"One of the first things I did upon arrival in Norway was to obtain a library card and use the down time to improve my language skills. The library was an important base where I could make bi-weekly visits and re-charge." - James M. Miller

---

TOP TIPS

I would like to end this chapter by giving you a general summary of my best advice for foreign job seekers in Norway. In the following chapters you can read about the different advice in more detail. But let us start your job seeker journey with you keeping the following in mind:

1. Learn Norwegian. This will be your key to finding a job in Norway.

2. Dare to stand out. Job seeking is all about selling yourself and standing out from the crowd.

3. Show up in person. Paying a personal visit to the

company or recruitment agency is the best policy when wanting to stand out.

4. Create a Norwegian language CV. As we will talk about, even though you do not yet speak Norwegian, it is vital to have a Norwegian version of your CV.

5. Build a network in Norway. And don't forget to use it!

6. Build an online presence. Like it or not, your future employer will search you out online. What will they find?

7. Get Norwegian references. Whether from voluntary work, training courses, part-time work or freelance projects, references rooted in Norway will carry more weight.

Finally yet perhaps most important of all, do not allow yourself to be stigmatised, by yourself or others. What do I mean by this? The most common negative attitude amongst foreign job seekers in Norway is based on an assumption that not having found a job has a direct connection to the fact that Norwegian employers do not want to hire you because you are a foreigner.

From experience I can tell you that this is rarely the case. Most foreign job seekers I have met have had trouble finding a job in Norway because they had not yet tried applying a more personal approach to their job seeking. Once they did, things changed, and they, sooner or later, ended up happily employed here in Norway.

Make sure you avoid being stuck with an attitude where you assume that your chance of getting a job in Norway is outside your own control. Such an attitude only serves to confirm itself. The less you think you can do, the less you will do, and surprise surprise, the less results you see.

Successfully finding a job in Norway is entirely up to you and the effort you put in.

CHAPTER EIGHT

DAVID

As Ingrid pointed out in the last chapter, many job seekers start their search online, but a lot less succeed. So does this mean you should skip the online search completely and throw yourself into personal networking? Hold on just a minute.

First of all, online job hunting is a fantastic way to research your chosen field. People email me all the time asking if there are jobs in their chosen field in their chosen city. Searching online tells you the answer.

It also helps you establish what Norwegian employers are looking for in your particular field. If the job advert is written in Norwegian, you can expect Norwegian language to be a requirement. Many job advertisements are published in English, but say that 'English and Norwegian' are required. I have found that this isn't always the case, but only if you meet all the other criteria and can offer some extremely relevant skills and/or experience.

In short: If the job advertisement is in English, it's worth an application. If it's in Norwegian, best not to bother.

Searching online also helps you find relevant contacts. While I don't recommend emailing any person you find mentioned in every job advert (that's a sure fire way to get blacklisted!), it can be beneficial to reach out to selected people as the starting point to building your own hyper-targeted professional network. Here's an example email:

"Hi Hilde, I'm a British project manager currently living in Oslo and working for Aker Solutions. I'm moving to Trondheim next month and would love to meet some people in the energy industry so I can get up to speed on things in Trondheim. Perhaps you would have time for a coffee and a chat sometime next month? If not, can you recommend any networking events or meetups that I could join? Thanks so much. David"

This kind of approach can work very well in Norway, but you shouldn't expect too many replies. Make sure you don't contact people with an expectation that they reply, as that can appear aggressive. Remember, you are asking someone who has no idea who you are for a favour. In the email above, my aim is to find out which networking events are most important in the Trondheim energy industry. In the email I've given Hilde an easy 'out', which is the thing I'm really looking for. If she accepts my invitation for a coffee, even better!

WHERE TO LOOK ONLINE

The biggest online jobs board in Norway by quite some distance is at Finn.no. The website is only available in Norwegian, but English language jobs are also posted. If you aren't yet confident in the Norwegian language, you can run the website through Google Translate by copy-pasting the URL into the Norwegian box and clicking translate. This works on desktops, tablets and smartphones in the browser, but not in the Google Translate app. Just remember that machine translation is not perfect!

Another large job board is the one provided by the Norwegian Labour and Welfare Administration at Nav.no. These listings are dominated by Norwegian language listings but there is an occasional gem to be found.

Beyond the two websites, I keep an updated feed of English language jobs collected from different sources on my website. As with the services provided by Finn and Nav, use it as a starting point for your research.

Aside from these general job board, many companies do advertise positions directly on their own careers webpages. In the chapter on Norway's top employers, we provided the links to these web pages where appropriate. Find all the relevant pages to your target employers, bookmark them and check them regularly.

Depending on your industry of choice, it may be worth registering your CV with recruitment agencies. In Norway there are general recruitment agencies such as Manpower, and ones that specialise in specific industries, such as the oil and gas industry. Many large companies use global recruitment firms for some or all of their hiring, but this is very industry- and company-specific.

Finally, LinkedIn is popular enough in Norway that it's worth spending some time updating your profile. A top tip from me: Make it clear in your one-line bio that you are looking for work and what it is you do. It's difficult to do this in one line, but it can be done! Here are a few examples:

- "Award-winning graphic designer in Oslo for hire"
- "Do you need PR services in Stavanger?"
- "Experienced, creative chef available now in Bergen"

And so on. It's generally fine to use English on your LinkedIn profile as many Norwegians do, but try to write personal messages in Norwegian if you can. At least a line or two can make all the difference when it comes to a positive impression. If after some research you find a lot of relevant people on LinkedIn, it could be worth investing in a premium membership, which allows you to email people directly that you are not already connected to, and gives you access to a very handy advanced search function.

"If you have technical expertise then get your CV on Finn.no and recruiters will call you (at least in Oslo). I found that even though my CV was in English and it was obvious that I wasn't Norwegian the people contacting me would speak in Norwegian, so it obviously still helps get your foot in the door to speak the language even if the

company is willing to accommodate someone who
isn't yet fluent." - Cristina

As has been hinted at several times already in this book,
relying on the internet to find a job in Norway is not the
best idea. For some people it works wonders, but others
should just consider the internet as nothing more than a
starting point for their job research, and of course as a tool
for networking.

Now I'm going to hand things over to Ingrid, who has years
of expertise in helping foreign job seekers get away from the
computer screen and in front of real people who are looking
to hire!

Useful resources:

- Finn: https://www.finn.no/job/browse.html
- Nav: https://tjenester.nav.no/stillinger/
- Life in Norway:
  https://www.lifeinnorway.net/jobs/

CHAPTER NINE
LOOKING IN PERSON

INGRID

As a job seeker in Norway, foreign or Norwegian, you will most likely experience that you apply for a position and then might not hear anything back. If you stick to the job seeker strategy that only implies sitting at home in front of the computer applying to open positions via email, there is a big chance you will not see any results. I have met many, many job seekers who have tried this for several years without result. Only when they realise that they have to get out of the house they start to see results.

This chapter then, is most likely the most important chapter in this book. To find a job in Norway you have to get out of your house and start to talk to people in person. Here, we will look at two important ways of doing this; one - through networking and two - through applying for positions in person. Let us start by looking at just how important professional networking is in Norway.

Life in Norway Survey: Was your job formally
advertised?

41.7%: Yes

58.3%: No

THE IMPORTANCE OF NETWORKING

The importance of networking in a job seeker situation may
vary some depending on where you are situated in Norway,
however in Trondheim it is for sure the most important
effort you can make to find a job. There are two reasons to
why it is so important:

Firstly, several open positions are never posted online, as the
employer prefers to look in his or hers network to see if
someone fits the requirements.

Secondly, as we will talk about further down, when a position is posted online, the hardest part is to stand out
amongst other qualified candidates. One of the very best
ways of doing this is if you know someone who also works
there or someone who knows the employer and can recommend you to him/her.

Networking in Norway might seem a bit different from
other countries, where networking normally translates into
talking to people who hold power in some way or another.
When talking about networking in Norway, I would like to
invite you to open up your mind and try to think of
networking in a broader sense than the one stated above.
Because Norway is socially an egalitarian society, we under-

stand the workplace as an organisation where everyone involved should be able to voice their opinion.

Therefore, the boss of the company will take it into consideration if a junior coworker gives a recommendation about who to hire. Which means that you do not have to actually know the manager to be considered for a position – it might be enough that you know someone who knows the manager – either employee or friend/family. That being said, Norwegians do not always feel comfortable recommending someone for a position, and they normally need to feel a certain degree of closeness to the person to do so.

Networking then, can be anything where you meet people and create relationships with them. It can be a straight up professional networking event, or it can be any social event where you meet and talk to new people. The main point is that if many people know of you and what kind of job you are looking for, your chances of hearing about a relevant position and for someone to recommend you for, will multiply. As mentioned earlier, Norwegians are not good at doing small talk with strangers on the bus, but if you look for organised activity, you are much more likely to meet people that are more open. In addition, of course, you do not need to network only with Norwegians!

> "Get out and network. Even do some work for free to prove your skills if you have no prior experience in Norway. If you want to be in a startup you need to prove yourself as a "potato": versatile." - Kim S.

NETWORKING TIPS

Even though networking in a broader sense can be anything where you meet other people, I do recommend that you try to be strategic in your choices on how to network. Look for events and activities that are in some way related to your line of work – if possible. Events that are directly related to work life is more effective than for example your Norwegian class, where everyone else also are job seekers. Let us go through some examples on how you can do networking in Norway:

Participate in a voluntary project: Not only does this help you to get to know new people, it is also positive for your CV. By adding a current project to your CV, you avoid holes and might be able to get a good work reference that is valuable to have for any future job interview. Getting yourself out of the house and activated is also good for morale and can boost your job seeker motivation – being a job seeker can become lonely and take its toll on your positive attitude. In this sense, any voluntary project will be good. There are different organisations that ask for volunteers, from Red Cross to film or music festivals around the country. Remember that voluntary work is also work – engage yourself as you would for a paid job and make sure you follow through on what you have promised. If it is a possibility to get a new work reference then make sure you leave a great impression.

Attend professional networking events: Professional networking events are being held on a weekly basis in all the biggest cities in Norway, so chances are you will find something relevant for you. I recommend starting by looking up the chamber of commerce in your city, and by trying to contact any workers union or organisation related to your line of work. This will be a good start to figure out what networking events you should do.

Through the chamber of commerce, you will most likely have to pay to participate. As a job seeker you are probably careful when spending money, but I recommend that you think of the entrance fee as an investment that will heighten your chances of finding employment. Much like buying some new clothes for the job interview. Another good way of finding professional networking events is by following the social media pages of companies that interest you – it is common that companies arrange breakfast events for example that are open for anyone interested.

Find relevant social events: There are also events arranged in the afternoons for people who share the same interests, this can be both hobby based interests or professional ones.

For example, is your line of work connected to environmental issues? Then Green Drinks is an international concept where people who care about the environment get together and talk and have drinks. This event is currently being held in both Tromsø, Bergen, Stavanger, Oslo and Trondheim. Google "green drinks + city of choice" and see what you can find!

Another way of finding group activities that you find relevant is by checking out meetup.com, or by doing some research on facebook and other social media.

Have a coffee: Even though Norwegians sometimes come across as if they are not the most social beings (especially if you yourself come from a more outgoing culture) some of us still like to connect with others and like getting to know new people.

I therefore recommend directly contacting people who does something similar to you or already seem to work at your dream company. Not everyone is up for, or have time to, sitting down for a coffee with someone they do not know, but it is well worth the try to ask them anyway. You might get a yes and the person might end up being a valuable contact for you in the future – or you to them.

Here I would advise you to use LinkedIn actively to contact the person, but it is also possible to call or email them. Another way to contact someone could be to go to events where you think this person might also go. Use the coffee meeting as a way of getting to understand better the job market in your field, and avoid asking direct favours as you might come off as too pushy.

Ask for help: Sometimes, asking for help can be hard to do and it can be difficult to know how to ask. Norwegians can also be hard to read, and sometimes we do not offer our help even though it might seem natural to do so.

You will see this when you try to push two suitcases, a dog, a baby carriage and a baby into a bus (there is a big chance no one offers to help you – not even the bus driver). Maybe we Norwegians worry too much that we will bother the other person, or we think the other person will get offended thinking we implied that they were not able to do it themselves.

I once assisted a German job seeker who had worked as a lawyer in his home country. When he moved to Norway he soon realised that his landlord was also a lawyer. This seemed like a great opportunity to get some help on how to jumpstart his Norwegian career.

He assumed that the property owner would offer his help, since he knew that his tenant also was a lawyer, but nothing happened. In the end the job seeker decided to send an email and ask if the landlord could throw him any advice on how to find a job. For some reason the landlord needed a direct request before he was comfortable offering his help. From then on, he helped the job seeker get interviews and showed him where to apply.

Blogging: Another good way of creating a relevant network for yourself is by offering your services as a guest blogger, or by starting your own blog where you collaborate with others.

This is particularly a good idea if the blog is related to your field of work – this way you get to know others who work with the same issues and you stand out from the crowd by making a name for yourself as an authority in your field. It is very likely that a future employer will google your name once you have been to a job interview, and showing that you are sincerely engaged in the issues concerning your line of work can be a great advantage.

I was connected with an architecture firm in advance through connections with my girlfriend's family who were able to show the company my online portfolio and c.v without involving me. Having a mutual connection meant everything and I found that in a smaller town like Bodø, they were crying out for young architects at the time (and probably still are now) as most young graduates prefer the glamour of the bigger cities. So my advice is to make the most of any connection you may have no matter how vague, as it really is who you know. Don't write off the smaller places outside Oslo and Bergen break the trend and you might find the smaller cities can't attract enough young workers." - Matt

---

APPLY IN PERSON

When you apply for an open position at a company, you will have to assume that there are from 60 to 100 other applicants also applying for the same position. In a few cases there are less applicants, and in some cases even many more than a hundred, but it is safe to say that normally there are at least 60 other applications and CVs being considered.

As we talk about in the chapter about job interviews in Norway, it is also safe to assume that only five to ten applicants get the call for the interview. My experience is that most job seekers see the ad for the position and say "I'm 100 % qualified, I will get an interview for sure!"

Then they do not receive any news about the position until it gets given to someone else. So, what happened?

Here, the logical way of thinking for most is to assume that they were in fact not qualified, or even worse, some go down the path of assuming that it has something to do with racism and the fact that they are not Norwegian.

In such cases, the answer is probably much more simple: More than 10 applicants were just as qualified for the position as you yourself were, and the employer had to make a choice as to whom they would call for the interview. If more than ten applicants were equally qualified, how do they figure out which ones to call?

This is why showing up in person is so important: it is vital that you do something more than just send the application and CV via internet to show interest, to make sure that you stand out of the crowd.

The best way of standing out is by showing more interest than the average applicant shows, and the easiest and most effective way of showing your enthusiasm is by showing up personally at the company where you want to work. This does not only show that you are eager to work there, but also it is a possibility to give your future employer a much broader first impression of you than what you papers can do. Let us look at how and when is the best time to show up in person.

The best timing for showing up in person is before you actually apply for the position – this way you can go talk to the contact person for the position and ask relevant questions about the content of the job. It is also a good idea to call if you cannot show up personally, and call after the deadline to ask how the process is going.

The main point here is to make sure the employer notices you and sees that you are very interested in the position. This also goes for positions that managed by recruitment agencies. In this case, it is the recruitment agent you have to convince, so make sure you show up in person at the recruitment agency to express your interest.

That being said, I recommend that you use the trial and

error method when it comes to what you say and how you act.

Showing up personally without an appointment or interview can be nerve-wracking to say the least, but it will most likely be the number one most effective thing you do to make sure you get yourself to the job interview. Showing up in person might very well come across as bold, but it will also show your employer that you take initiative, that you go for what you really want and that you encounter scary situations with courage.

Give yourself a big pat on the back afterwards for doing everything in your power to find a career and life you love here in Norway. Well done!

CHAPTER TEN
REALLY LEARN NORWEGIAN

INGRID

The number one most important skillset job seekers in
Norway must develop is most definitely the Norwegian
language.

Since many Norwegians speak English and do not mind
using it, it is easy for a newly arrived foreigner to assume
that English will suffice in professional life here as well.
This is normally not the case, and studies show that the
biggest reason why employers doubt hiring foreigners is
their lack of Norwegian skills.

As the Topplederundersøkelsen 2014 survey showed, 86
percent of Norwegian company leaders say that the most
important reason why they choose not to hire a foreigner is
that they lack Norwegian language skills. 78 percent of the
leaders also stated that the lack of Norwegian skills make it
harder for foreigners in the company to make the most of
their credentials.

In most cases, an employer will expect that the job seeker

speaks Norwegian. There are some exceptions to this, like for example if the company is multinational and tend to hire specific professionals from abroad. In some cases, the company hires more foreigners than Norwegians, which makes English the natural work language.

But this is rare, and I do not recommend counting on finding a job in these few companies, unless you already know that your skillset is highly sought after in Norway and that companies that seek your skills tend to hire from abroad.

This used to be the case for oil and gas companies in Norway, since for many years, there was a shortage of engineers to work in this field. However, in the last couple of years these companies have let go of many workers. Now that there is no longer a shortage of professionals in this field, the companies have the possibility to hire workers who speak Norwegian.

Normally the logic goes like this: if the company can hire employees who speak Norwegian, they will. If there are Norwegian speakers who have the same skillset as you applying for the same position as you, then you are at a disadvantage if you do not speak Norwegian. If there are no applicants who speak Norwegian applying for the same position as you, you will most likely be more competitive.

This does not mean that a company that has Norwegian as its work language does not hire foreigners nor that they do not hire workers who do not speak Norwegian.

In a few cases, a company will hire a foreigner under an agreement that the employee will over time become fluent in Norwegian. The company then also tries to adapt the work environment to the person who does not speak Norwegian by using English during staff meetings. This is not common, so I wouldn't recommend basing your job-seeking strategy on this alone.

THE IMPORTANCE OF SPEAKING NORWEGIAN

As a foreigner moving to Norway, your first impression might be that most Norwegians speak English. When you visit the grocery store you find that the employees switch with ease to English when speaking to you. Why then do Norwegian employers find it so important that their employees speak Norwegian?

There are several reasons for this, one of them being that Norwegians normally speak Norwegian among themselves. Therefore, even though a staff meeting will be held in English, once your Norwegian colleagues start individual conversations, they will switch over to Norwegian again.

During lunch break, the conversation will most likely be in Norwegian, and many times your colleagues will not keep in mind that you do not speak Norwegian and rarely someone will ask everyone to switch to English so that you can partake in the conversation. Group emails might also be in Norwegian.

Basically if there are more Norwegians working at your company than foreigners, any communication that is not directly aimed at you will be in Norwegian. For an employer, there's a natural concern that you would miss important information.

Another important reason as to why employers prefer that you speak Norwegian is the company's customers and suppliers, since these also normally speak Norwegian and don't necessarily want to speak English.

The conclusion is that most communication in the Norwegian work environment is in Norwegian, and the use of English is mostly an exception.

"Learn Norwegian as soon as possible, or make sure you are such a rare unicorn that they simply can't do without you. After that, start learning Norwegian anyway. I'm sure you have your "what if" moments, such as "What if I invested 1,000 dollars in Facebook/Google/Bitcoin/that start-up that was so promising five years ago, how would my life be now?" Well, knowing Norwegian when you are out looking for a job is basically that Facebook/Google/Bitcoin investment from five years ago. It will make such a difference in being able to access a good job and open new opportunities. There is no other way to having access to medium/higher income levels and future job opportunities in general." - Lucian

---

HOW TO LEARN NORWEGIAN

Our best advice is to start learning Norwegian as soon as you know that you are moving to Norway. There are online courses that you can take, and private tutors who offer

Norwegian classes via Skype. Once you know when you will arrive here, start looking into when and where Norwegian classes are being held, and sign up as soon as possible.

There are private language schools in most cities, and you might be able to take Norwegian classes at the public university without enrolment as a student, although they normally have a longer application process than other Norwegian classes. Also, many local municipalities offer Norwegian classes for foreigners.

Remember, it's a marathon, not a sprint. Language learning is a 'step' process. You'll make little breakthroughs along the way, such as your first conversation in a coffee bar, the first time you complete a conversation with a Norwegian who doesn't feel the need to switch to English, the first time you understand a newspaper story, the first time you complete a phone conversation in Norwegian, and so on.

But making these steps can be tough. It can often feel like you're making no progress until you achieve one of these 'steps', but in reality you're making progress every time you study, and every time you speak.

Mix things up: Don't just rely on one book or one course. The best way to learn any language is to absorb as much material as you can in as many forms as possible.

Remember that a language isn't just about reading! Norwegian TV, YouTubers, NRK podcasts, online newspapers, apps, and films are all great ways to mix up your language learning.

If you're starting out, try the *Klar Tale* online newspaper and podcast, written and spoken in simple Norwegian.

Volunteering: As most foreigners in Norway have experienced, it is not so easy to chat up a stranger on the street, as many Norwegians find it awkward to engage in small talk with strangers.

Norwegian social codes makes it a bit of a challenge to practice your dialect skills, but it is still not impossible. Norwegians tend to be more open and willing to get to know strangers when they are participating in organised activity.

For example, when they are at the work place, socialising is seen as natural and necessary, the same with organised sports activities, the neighbourhood 'dugnad' or a parent – teacher meeting at the children's school. Therefore, a good way to practice your Norwegians skills and to create a bigger network, could be by, for example, volunteering at your nearest 'Frivillighetssentralen' (Volunteering Centre), at the next festival in your city, or at the nearest public cabin, or maybe at the library.

Attend local language cafes: Go to language cafes as often as you can, and whenever you do talk to someone Norwegian, make sure that you do not freeze up and switch to English. If the other person switches to English, remember that he or she most likely does it to make you feel more comfortable. It is perfectly fine if you just stick with Norwegian even though the other person tries to switch to English.

By the way, are you fluent in another language? If so, it might be a good idea to find a speaker of that language who is studying at the nearest university and ask if they would like to be your language buddy.

DIALECTS

Most foreigners tell me that they find it hard to understand Norwegians outside of the classroom.

The problem here is that most Norwegian classes for foreigners, both private and public, only focus on 'bokmål', which is one of two written languages in Norway – the other one being 'nynorsk'. Bokmål as a written language derives from the south of Norway, and is pretty similar to the spoken language in the city of Oslo and the surrounding area (even though it is not completely the same – Oslo also has its dialect words, but many words are the same as 'bokmål').

'Nynorsk' is a written language unifying all of the Norwegian dialects by sampling words from most of them. As a foreigner, your class will most likely only focus on 'bokmål'.

The biggest newspapers in Norway are all written in 'bokmål', and the same goes for most books printed. Therefore, if you are residing in Oslo or in the close proximity, you might not consider the dialect to be a big challenge once you are practicing your Norwegian skills outside the classroom.

However, if you happen to be living in any other part of Norway, you will probably find that there are sometimes big differences between the language you are learning in class and the way people around you speak. Many words in the Norwegian dialects are completely different from 'bokmål', and it is common in some dialects to shorten down verbs, for example "Jeg spiser" in 'bokmål', translates in the Trondheim area to "Æ spis". Or might just be traded for the verb 'å eta' which is not used at all in 'bokmål'. Then the sentence in the Trondheim area would be 'Æ et'. Pretty confusing, right?

As most foreigners who attended my services in Trondheim tells me, their language confidence takes an abrupt skydive once they are outside of class. They go to class, practice with the other pupils and the teacher, read and speak 'bokmål', and feel like they are starting to master a simple conversation, like for example at the grocery store. Then, once they are at the counter at the local grocery store, they feel like the other person is speaking a completely new language.

Do not despair! It is completely possible to learn the local dialect but it just requires some extra patience and time. By practicing every day you will be fluent in both 'bokmål' and 'bergensk' or ' stavangersk' or 'nordlæning' or (fill in the blank) in no time at all! The crucial thing here is that you are able to understand the local dialect. Nobody minds if you then speak in a more neutral Norwegian similar to bokmål.

My best tip is to find ways to engage with the locals so that you can practice speaking and listening to the local dialect.

Do some research as to what you think will be the best fit for you. Just make sure you get on this as your number one priority when relocating to Norway.

Useful resources:

- The Mystery of Nils:
  https://www.lifeinnorway.net/go/nils
- Norwegian Class 101:
  https://www.lifeinnorway.net/go/norwegian101

- Klar Tale: http://www.klartale.no/

So, you've started to network either online or in person (preferably both!), learned basic Norwegian, and found some job advertisements that interest you. What's next? It's time to whip your CV (resume) into shape.

Most foreign job seekers I have met in Norway are highly qualified workers, which means that they hold at least a bachelors degree from college or university, and some even hold a PhD. A logical way of thinking, when you already are highly educated, is to assume that you know how to write a good CV.

What most foreign job seekers do not take into account though, is that a Norwegian CV almost certainly looks different from their home country's CV. The differences that appear in the Norwegian CV are cultural ones, and reflect attitudes and ethics that we can find in the Norwegian work environment. If you lack prior work experience in Norway, it could be hard to guess what these differences are.

It's important to take the time to make sure your CV meets the Norwegian standards. Being a job seeker is about selling yourself as a highly qualified employee, and a part of this is to show your future employer that you know and understand Norwegian cultural norms, which indicates you are likely to get along well with your new Norwegian colleagues.

Remember though, that as cultural tendencies always change, so does a standard Norwegian CV. The following advice is based on how a Norwegian CV typically looks in 2018, but people also tend to put their personal touches on a CV. Depending on their background and what job they are seeking, they might choose to leave some information out and include something else.

For example, if you are applying for a job as an accountant, how relevant would it necessarily be to let your future employer know that you have a PADI diving license? Maybe not so much. But what if you are applying for a position as an accountant at a Diving gear store? Then maybe yes, leaving it there will to show that your personal interests align with those of your future colleagues, which means that you might get along great with them, which again means that your personality will add to the positive work environment.

So with that in mind, here is how to write a Norwegian CV.

LANGUAGE

The first question you will ask yourself is almost certainly: Should I write my CV in Norwegian, even though I am not fluent yet? The answer is absolutely yes. Write your CV in Norwegian from the beginning.

The point here is simple. You want to show your future employer that you are not just eager to adapt to Norwegian culture, you are also interested in, and on your way to speaking Norwegian. Most employers appreciate the effort you show in wanting to learn Norwegian, this tells them that even though you are not yet fluent, you are likely to become fluent in a reasonable period of time.

If you know very little Norwegian, it might also be a good idea to have an English version of your CV. When you apply for a position, depending on your language skills and what language the ad of the position is written in, you might want to send both CV's, or just one of them.

If the job advertisement is from an international company and published in English, feel free to send your English CV with an English cover letter. If the advertisement is in Norwegian, then always send the Norwegian version of your CV.

If you are nervous about the quality of your written Norwegian, have a native check it over (another benefit of in-person networking) and perhaps also send your English CV. By doing this, you show that you are making an effort with the language and more importantly, you understand the importance of learning Norwegian.

ASSUME NOTHING

Bear in mind that any qualifications or experience earned abroad may well be unfamiliar to a Norwegian, so your CV may need some extra explanation to ensure a prospective employer properly understands your background.

For example, I once read a foreign engineer's CV, and was immediately impressed with the work experience. This professional had worked with one of South America's biggest airlines, installing new software to their fleet of aeroplanes.

But, having lived for several years in South America, I have the necessary context to understand this person's professional background. A Norwegian employer who has never travelled to South America would most likely never have heard of this airline. In this instance, including a simple one-line explanation such as "South America's largest airline company" can make all the difference.

If there is something specific you wish to highlight, you can do so on the cover letter. For example, if you were selected for an exclusive study programme at your country's leading business school, explain why and the benefits you gained in your cover letter, not on your CV. This will help keep your CV clean, focused and easily scannable.

LENGTH OF CV

A normal CV in Norway is rarely longer than two pages, and can often be as short as one. This is because most employers get at least fifty job applications for each position they publish.

Since you are competing with at least fifty others, a short and sweet CV is the key to getting attention. If an employer is faced with five pages of text, consider how likely they are to spend the time searching for the most valuable information when there's a pile of shorter CVs underneath.

It should be easy for anyone to get a quick overview of your professional background in just a few seconds. Organisation is important to enable this. Use subheadings, keywords rather than long sentences and perhaps bold lettering for the most relevant information.

One exception to this rule is for academic CVs. These tend to follow a more international standard, which can be much longer because they normally contain a list of publication credits, amongst other things.

PHOTOGRAPH

There is always a discussion going on amongst career counsellors in Norway if job seekers should include a picture on their CV or not. The old, standard argument goes that you should not because you would not want your future employer to judge you based on looks, rather than your skills, but personally I strongly disagree with this.

I do not think a typical Norwegian employer cares if you could be a Miss Universe contestant or not. Most employers just want to make sure that you can do your job properly and that is what they are looking for in a CV.

By including a picture, you give a broader first impression since we as humans react better, and remember better, a visual image than just text. It is also not a bad idea to show the employer that you know how to dress and present yourself in a professional way.

If you choose to include a picture, use a neutral background, wear clothes you would wear to work and remember to smile! Avoid using pictures from social situations.

PERSONAL INFORMATION

The Norwegian CV always begins with general information, including:

- Home address (in Norway if you have one)
- Your Norwegian phone number
- Your email address
- Date of birth
- Nationality
- Website/blog (if you have one - especially relevant for creative positions)
- Family situation (married/single)

Make sure your web presence including your email address is professional. A Gmail address is fine as long as it's your name. Avoid the likes of cutecat84@hotmail.com that you used as a teenager! Google's Gmail service is seen as more professional in Norway compared to the likes of Hotmail or Yahoo, so it might be time to get a new email address. If you have a personal domain name, then all the better.

It is common to disclose your family situation in Norway, and many employers appreciate this. If you state that you are married with kids, it helps an employer to know you would fit in to the lunch hour conversations.

Since childcare rights are so well established in Norwegian work life, it is rare that any serious employer would see you having children as a disadvantage. This goes for both men and women.

KEY QUALIFICATIONS

Another important element to a professional Norwegian CV is known as *Nøkkelkvalifikasjoner* or Key Qualifications.

This is essentially space for a one or two-line summary of your main selling points. Like it or not, some employers will judge your candidacy based on this section alone. If they like what they read, your CV will go into a pile to be read in full.

I recommend that you change this sentence for each position you apply for to emphasise the most relevant information. Example: "Accountant with 5 years experience in international tax regulations at Schlumberger, one of the world's largest oilfield service companies."

WORK EXPERIENCE AND EDUCATION

The next step would be to add your professional experience and education. I would say that it is most common to start by listing your professional experience, starting with the most recent.

It is also common in Norway to list education first, so consider what you find to be most valuable depending on the position you are applying. Is it your experience or your education that makes you a great candidate for the job? Put that first.

For your education, it is common to state the title of your degree and then add the name of the university/college, and not the other way around. Example: "Master in Social Anthropology, University of Belfast, Ireland."

Remember to add the country where the university is situated at the end. This is not necessary if it is a Norwegian university, but otherwise you should add it since people's geography skills differ.

LANGUAGES, COURSES AND VOLUNTARY WORK

The next step would be to add what languages you speak, starting with your native language. I recommend using logical one-word descriptions of your level of fluency: native, fluent, advanced, intermediate, beginner.

I see many foreign job seekers in Norway writing "Norwegian – B1 level course finished". It can be a good thing to add that you are, or have attended Norwegian class, just to show that you are dedicated to learning Norwegian.

However, bear in mind that many Norwegian employers will not understand what B1 means. It's far better to use a descriptive word such as intermediate.

PERSONAL INTERESTS

It is common to add a little information about your personal interests in the CV, and it is normal that this is about your hobbies and favourite pastimes.

For example: skiing, hiking, football, cooking, knitting or anything that you enjoy that is not related to your professional life. Just be sure to keep it to keywords instead of long, descriptive sentences. After all, this is not a profile on a dating website!

REFERENCES

Having great references is critical. In Norway it is common for the employer to contact your references after you have been to an interview. They will contact your references if they find you to be one of the most relevant candidates for the position.

Being able to list at least one Norwegian reference is very important. Your future employer will feel more comfortable making a quick phone call to a fellow Norwegian, or being able to email someone in Norwegian. Imagine yourself making a phone call to a stranger on the other side of the planet.

Let's say you are an employer from the USA and will have to call up the candidate's references in China. You would probably be concerned if the person who answers doesn't speak English well. When should you call? How do you pronounce the person's name?

If you are new in Norway, keep your foreign professional references but ask your Norwegian teacher or someone you are doing voluntary work with if they would act as an additional reference. While not as solid as a professional reference, they can verify if you follow up on tasks, show up on time, your commitment level, and if you are generally reliable. It also shows the prospective employer that you are making an attempt to integrate into Norwegian society. Avoid listing friends or family in your reference list.

The best approach to including references on your CV is to write "referanser oppgis ved forespørsel" at the end of the document, which means "references are available upon request". When you attend the job interview, bring a piece of paper listing the references and contact information.

FINAL THOUGHTS

Personal traits are typically left for the cover letter. Remember to stay away from fluff words like: positive, hard worker, or outgoing when you describe yourself. It is common that you will be asked to email your cover letter and CV to the company when you apply, so use a logical name on the file, such as Ingrid_Fabrello_CV2018.doc.

Also remember to write a a short comment in the email, maybe copy and paste in your "key qualifications" here, so it's easy for the recipient to get a quick overview of who you are.

Emphasise any and all experience from Norway. Even if you have never been employed in Norway, it is always a positive to add any voluntary work or freelance projects that you have done. Also if that's what you are spending your days doing while on the job hunt, it helps to avoid question-able holes in your CV's timeline. For an employer it shows that you are eager to get to know your local community.

Remember that a CV should not be static. You can and should update it frequently and emphasise different details and experiences depending on the position.

Last but definitely not least: Have someone who knows Norwegian well, preferably a native, look through your CV before you send it. This will help to catch any little mistakes or a phrase that doesn't sound quite right.

As we have already talked about in the chapter on finding a job in person, it can be a frustratingly long process before you gain a chance at a job interview.

When you get the first call, give yourself a pat on the back. Standing out enough for an employer to take notice of you is a big step on the journey. Now, the real work begins.

The most common job interview in Norway normally lasts for at least one hour. You will most likely be the only candidate at the job interview, unless it is a group interview, which I'll talk about later.

The person interviewing you is most likely to be the person who will be your immediate manager if you get the position, but there may also be other people present. This can be a representative from the HR department, or other relevant people from the company.

It is difficult to know exactly who you can expect to be present, because it differs a lot from company to company, and depends on whether it is a private company or a government institution. However, in general, you can expect anything between one to four people present at the interview.

If there are several people present, it's likely that they will have agreed beforehand who will conduct the interview and ask the questions. If you notice during the interview that some of them do not interact with you as much, or not at all, there's no need to worry. Relax, safe in the knowledge that it's just part of the process, and not a reflection on their opinion of you!

Most employers also see the job interview as a situation in which you as a candidate have the chance to get to know more about the position. It is common for the interview to be divided into two parts. First, they will tell you more about the company and the position you have applied for, and then they will begin to ask you questions. In this second part, don't miss the opportunity to ask questions yourself. Employers expect you to want to know more about the place that you expect to be spending much of your time over the years to come.

Show a genuine interest, research the industry and its challenges, ask about how the company is meeting these challenges, and what you can do to help. If you don't show a genuine interest in the company and its fortunes, the interview panel may begin to wonder how serious you are about the position. Don't be shy about asking more personal questions too, such as if all employees eat lunch together. This will show that you care about the social sides to the job and that you would like to be a part of a positive work environment.

COMMON INTERVIEW QUESTIONS

Let's look at what kind of questions they might ask you during the interview. Let me clarify that there is no recipe for what questions you might get during a job interview, and the questions can differ a lot from interview to interview. My personal experience though, and also the experience of a lot of job seekers that I have counselled, shows that a high percentage of job interviews in Norway tend to include many of the same questions.

Before reading the list of possible questions, remember that no matter what they ask you during the interview, there is one overall question that the employer is trying to answer for themselves during the interview: "Why should I hire you?"

This question hides behind all the other questions that you get, and the first thing you should do when you start preparing for the interview, is to figure out what your answer is. Then, let your main arguments as to why they should hire you become a natural part of the answers you give.

Here is a good example on how to go about this. A common first question at a Norwegian job interview is something like: "So, tell us a little bit about yourself" Or: "So, who are you?"

This is not the time to start listing your favourite pastimes or your family situation. Because it is such broad question, it is easy to get lost in all the possible answers you can give. I highly recommend using this opportunity to emphasise your best selling points as to why they should hire you. Remember the 'Key Qualifications' summary on your CV.

Start the interview by emphasising these most relevant skills and experience, as if it were the only question you were going to be asked. The ideal situation is you say something so interesting that they immediately ask you for more.

Other possible questions include:

- Why did you apply for this position?
- What kind of work have you done before?
- Why did you quit your former job? / Why do you want to leave your current job?
- What are your best personal traits in a work situation?
- What did you do during the gaps in time on your CV
- Are you easily stressed? / How do you cope working under pressure?
- Do you prefer tasks that are routine or do you prefer new tasks all the time?
- What kind of tasks do you like the least?
- What are the most positive and negative things you can say about yourself?
- Do you prefer to work by yourself or in a team?
- What can you add to the position?
- What do you think will be the most challenging aspect of this position?
- Where do you see yourself working in five years?
- What is your current family situation?
- What salary do you currently have?
- What kind of salary do you expect?

The last three questions tend to concern foreign job seekers more than the rest. Some women are nervous about telling their potential future employer that they have a three-year-old child at home, because it might indicate a need to take more days off.

This is normally not something you need to worry about in Norway. As mentioned earlier in the book, Norwegians see childcare rights as an integral part of the Norwegian work life, and few serious employers will look upon children as a disadvantage. This can be difficult for those new to Norway to understand, but trust us!

When it comes to salary expectations, it might be difficult to come up with a figure if you have not yet worked in Norway. I recommend that you just answer that you expect to earn the Norwegian wage that is standard for your field of work. You do not need to give them a specific number if you do not know what that number should be.

The first interview is definitely not the time and place to start negotiating your salary, so the best thing to do is to wait until they offer you the position and send you the contract. That is normally when you find out what salary they will offer you, although they might also tell you during the interview. Before you accept the offer and sign the contract, it would be a good idea to ask someone who has some insight into your field of work if the salary is acceptable. If you find that it is not, then this would be the time to negotiate.

"I successfully negotiated an increase of 40,000 kroner on the annual salary I was offered simply by asking when the contract came through. Salary wasn't mentioned during the interview, but I had researched the industry standards beforehand so when the contract offer came through, I knew there would be room to negotiate." - David

---

For a typical first interview in Norway, the employer normally calls between five to ten candidates that they want to get to know better. From there, there might be a second and a third interview where they narrow it down to the most relevant candidates for the position.

Having said that, there might just be one round of interviews. It really depends on the job, the employer, and how much they feel they need to talk to the candidates before offering one of them the position.

Life in Norway Survey: How many interviews did you have?

69.4%: One

19.4%: Two

11.2%: Three or more

During a second or third interview, it is common to receive example tasks. You might get the task before you go to the interview so that you can prepare yourself, or you might get the task during the interview with no prior notification. The point is to see how you will deal with a given task, so the case question normally relates to the types of tasks you will get once you are working at the company. If you get the case sent to you before the interview, prepare your answers well and take some time to make a brief presentation, even if you've not been asked for one.

GROUP INTERVIEWS

Some employers choose to use other types of job interviews when they are hiring, such as speed interviews or group interviews. Both interview types are usually followed by a more typical one-to-one interview, if the candidate makes the cut after the first interview round.

A group interview usually consists of up to six candidates who take turns answering questions, and may possibly be given tasks to work on together. If placed in a group interview situation, try to ignore the answers of everyone else and focus on giving the best impression of yourself.

If the group is asked to discuss a topic, it may be that the employers are watching how you interact with others and your ability to work as part of a team. If so, allow others the chance to speak, don't interrupt, and try to bring the quieter members of the group into the conversation. During a Norwegian meeting it is important for everyone to have their say, so doing this shows you understand this important cultural norm.

A speed interview is a short interview of 10 to 20 minutes, during which time they might ask you to make a presentation that you prepared in advance.

Perhaps the most common question asked by foreign job seekers about Norwegian job interviews is whether they will be expected to speak Norwegian at the interview.

This is an important question, and one I recommend taking into consideration no matter what your language level is at the time of the interview. As I have mentioned earlier in this book, speaking Norwegian is without a doubt the main key to unlocking your professional possibilities in Norway. I therefore recommend that you start practicing and mentally preparing for doing a job interview in Norwegian, no matter how challenging it sounds.

A job interview is a stressful enough situation as it is, and conducting it in your second or third language will add to the stress. The point here is not that you have to be fluent in Norwegian before you go to the interview, but rather to show that you are on the path to learning Norwegian and interested in Norwegian culture. You must be able to demonstrate that you understand that to successfully integrate into Norwegian society you need to speak the language, and the only way you can do that is by making an effort with speaking the language.

If you're a beginner, even speaking just a little Norwegian at the interview will go a long way towards showing this understanding. If you've been honest about your level of Norwegian in your application, speak some Norwegian in the interview and then ask to switch to English if you feel the need. As long as you start in Norwegian, this shouldn't be looked upon too unfavourably.

If you have stated in your CV that you have an intermediate

Norwegian speaking level, and then show up at the job interview and ask to speak English from the beginning, you will leave a bad impression.

Firstly, it makes it look like you have been dishonest on your CV. Secondly, it is hard to come off as sincere if you say that you are a fast learner and that you adapt well to a new work environment if you have lived for years in Norway but have not yet tried to learn the language.

The key here is to set expectations, and then meet those expectations. Any intent to speak Norwegian at the job interview will be appreciated. It is much better to say some sentences in Norwegian and then ask to switch to English, than to not speak any Norwegian at all. Don't worry, there are many people who have been in the same shoes.

Put the effort in, and in no time at all you will be a fluent Norwegian speaker!

SOCIAL NORMS

Now that we've got the formal stuff out of the way, it's time to look at some of the more subtle elements of a job interview in Norway. If you've not been in Norway for long you may not appreciate the social norms that exist in Norwegian society. Few places can these be seen more than in a job interview.

Do not be late: This is the most important social code to keep in mind when you are preparing for a Norwegian job interview. Norwegians are extremely punctual compared to many other nationalities, and a surefire way to avoid getting a job offer would be to show up even just five minutes past the agreed meeting time. If the job interview starts at 10am, be there no later than 9.50am. If you show up at 10.05, you are officially late for the interview and have most likely blown any chances of getting the position.

Excuses won't help. The day before the interview, travel to the offices to confirm their location and the time it takes to get there. If you see that your chosen bus gets you to the office five minutes before the interview starts, don't take the chance, take the earlier bus the next day.

The best plan is to arrive near the location half-an-hour before the interview starts and wait nearby. That way you won't need to rush and can relax, read through your notes, and still arrive in good time for the interview.

Body language: Most job seekers assume that they know what a positive body language entails, but there can sometimes be some cultural differences involved that it's smart to study and take into consideration. Different cultures can have different understandings of how you show respect with your body language.

For example, in Norway it is normal to smile during a job interview. In some countries, smiling might represent a lack of respect for the person interviewing you. It is also normal to shake the person's hand and to say your name once you meet with them. You can also add "hyggelig" afterwards, which in this context translates as "pleased to meet you".

When you're seated, avoid crossing your arms as it can seem like you have a standoffish attitude. My experience is that some people cross their arms as a way of feeling more comfortable in a stressful social situation, but it does not come across as very open and interested in a formal Norwegian setting.

Also, do not feel shy about making some small talk before the interview starts. Small talk can help to combat any stress you may be feeling, while at the same time giving an impression of you as a relaxed and sociable person.

Clothing: What is considered appropriate work attire changes from workplace to workplace, and also from place to place in Norway. That being said, work attire tends to be somewhat relaxed in Norway compared to other countries.

It is hard to generalise, but I would say that it is not as common for people to wear a suit to work, as it would be in some other countries.

My best advice is to research the workplace first. Try searching for employees that work there or look them up on LinkedIn, which might give you an idea of the level of formality.

Also, remember that work attire changes from city to city, even within the same company. Therefore, the company's branch office in Trondheim might require less formal attire than the same company's head office in Oslo. Remember that it is also considered normal to show up a bit more formal for a job interview than for everyday work.

One thing I also ask foreign job seekers in Norway to consider for the job interview is their shoes and outerwear. Even though the weather in Norway invites you to wear mountain gear every day, it is a good idea to make an effort both with the choice of jacket and shoes for a job interview.

Unless there is a snowstorm outside, try to avoid looking as if you are on your way to a mountain hike immediately after the interview.

Enthusiasm: Something I often see that foreign job seekers misinterpret at a Norwegian interview is the possibility to show that you really want the position. For many cultures, the job interview is a formal situation where the employer has called you in to verify that you have the professional skills that you have stated in your CV.

At a Norwegian interview, I suggest you think of it more as a meeting where the employer has called you in to see whether you are a good fit. It's a subtle but very important difference.

Trusting that people are honest and truthful is typical Norwegian behaviour. This attitude extends to the job interview, where the focus is often not about verifying your skills and experience, but rather to see if your personality will fit into the specific work environment.

The employer wants to know what type of person you are and what attitude you will bring to work with you every day. If you are enthusiastic about the position, do not assume that the employer takes this for granted. Make sure you let them know that this is your dream job! This tells the employer that you will do your best to add positive value to the company and the work environment.

"At my first job interview, I spent more than half the time answering questions about my Life in Norway website. The two managers interviewing me had clearly made up their mind about my suitability for the role based on the application and references, and were using the interview simply to get to know me and decide if and how I would fit in. Once I realised that, the interview flew by and turned into a very casual conversation.

PREPARATION

To fully prepare yourself for an interview, research the company as much as you can. The internet is your friend here. Have they been in the news lately, or issued any press releases? This tells you what the current priorities are.

If you know the name of the hiring manager and/or the person who will be interviewing you, have they been interviewed in the media recently? What did they say?

Go through the list of common interview questions listed earlier in the chapter, and practice your answers. Try to think of a couple of examples you can use. This will help enormously for preparing to answer in Norwegian, as if your mind blanks on one example, you can simply switch to another.

Do not skip the hardest questions. Always have something to say about your weaknesses so you aren't forced to come with something on the spot. If you wait until the pressure of an interview to think about your weaknesses, what you say is unlikely to be as good as it could be.

Remember: Try not to think about the job interview as an exam! You are also there to figure out if it is the right position and company for you, and Norwegians absolutely understand that. Perhaps more so than any other country , a Norwegian job interview is a conversation.

Also remember to bring printed copies of your CV and

references, certified copies of your diplomas, and certificates from relevant courses you have completed.

AFTER THE INTERVIEW

At the interview itself, ask when you can expect to hear from them. This won't be seen as rude, it's simply you wanting to find out more about the process. It will also save you from nervously staring at your phone for weeks.

The day after the interview, send an email to thank the employer for the opportunity and to tell him/her that after learning more about the position you are now even more convinced that it is the right position for you. If, in fact, that is the case! Offer to answer any follow-up questions they might have.

When I ran Kulturkoordinator, I made sure to hold exit interviews with people as they left the course.

Although the Kulturkoordinator program no longer exists, there's still plenty of useful information contained within these stories.

With their permission, I've republished a couple here to give you a feel for how the 'start-to-finish' job search might work for you.

INTERVIEW WITH KAROLINA

Finding a job when moving from Poland to Norway was a harder task than Karolina had expected.

She moved to Trondheim almost 5 years ago, when her husband secured a PhD position at SINTEF. After finishing her master's degree in Cultural Studies in Poland, she never thought that it would take her two and a half years before she would find employment here. Karolina now works fulltime as a PhD candidate at NTNU.

What is the most important thing you have learned about job seeking in Norway?

The most important thing about job seeking in Norway is that you need to be really proactive in your efforts. Building a network is a prerequisite to finding meaningful employment. I would really recommend trying to establish some contacts before moving to Norway, and then participate in networking events and other relevant open meetings.

What had you been doing wrong in your job search?

I came from a system where sending a CV and motivational letter to an advertised position was enough, so I basically copied this approach here in Norway. That was a mistake.

As I mentioned before, looking for a job in Norway is a more "action-oriented" process. One has to be prepared to present oneself personally to a company of interest or attend relevant networking events, for example. Sending a CV and motivational letter is by far the least successful approach here!

How has starting to work here in Norway changed your everyday life?

First of all, working or studying is by far the best way to get integrated into the society. I have met a lot of interesting people and learned a lot about local mentality. There is so much more to Norway then skiing and brunost!

If you never made the changes you did to your job search, where would you be today?

I would most probably have felt defeated and moved somewhere else. When you are in a new country with a cultural code you don't entirely understand, and look for a job without success for a long time, it is very easy to build up a great dose of prejudice and anger. That in turn "blinds" you to your own potential mistakes, and you become less and less effective in the job search.

I think that the most important thing before starting to look for a job is to have a good plan. Know what you want to do and do thorough research on possibilities in the place you move to. Start acting as soon as possible.

I think that sometimes you just have to "dare" to do more, try new things and get out of your comfort zone. You have to be patient and be "out there" in order to meet people, to learn the cultural code.

What do you do at your PhD position at NTNU?

In my PhD position I do research on entrepreneurship education and how more students can become entrepreneurial. Apart from the research part, my work also involves participation in courses. I also have some practical obligations like organising workshops on entrepreneurship for various students groups and supervising master theses.

What is your best advice to foreigners looking for a job in Norway?

Be proactive, meet as many people as possible, get out and network, make a plan and stay positive. If there are any specialised companies or counselling services regarding job seeking in a place you move, use them as soon as possible after moving in.

Caroline moved with her family from Belgium to Norway three years ago, and after some tough years adjusting to life in Trondheim, she has now finally found her dream job.

She works as the coordinator of the HomeStart programme at the municipality of Melhus, just outside Trondheim.

Here she talks about how she finally landed the perfect job for her, and what she has learned about being a foreign job seeker in Norway.

Why did you move to Norway?

I moved to Norway because my husband got a permanent position as an associate professor at NTNU. We moved here with our three children; one is still in kindergarten, and the other two have started school.

What is your professional background?

I have a bachelor's degree in family sciences, which resembles the Norwegian title 'barnevernspedagog' (youth health worker). I worked several years in different patient organisations, first with organisational work.

After a while, I also started working more directly with families who struggled with chronic diseases. I have also been working as a volunteer myself in the same type of organisation as HomeStart, in Belgium (called DOMO), where I recruited other volunteers to join the program, which is the same as what I am doing now in my position as coordinator at the Melhus municipality.

Could you tell us more about what you do in your current position?

I really do a lot. I promote the family program HomeStart. The program offers help to families that have problems related to stress, and who need practical help together with emotional help in their daily life. It is actually a program that prevents problems from getting worse, helping the families before they are not able to cope anymore.

Participation is free for the families, and my position as coordinator is paid through the municipality. The Home-Start program is nationwide, and we have over 30 programs all over Norway. As the coordinator, it is my responsibility to recruit companies and coach volunteers for the program.

How was your experience of looking for a job in Norway?

Difficult! I had been trying to find a job for more than two years with little to no success at all. First, I tried to find a job in my field as a youth health worker, which was almost impossible, because there was a lot of competition. I was competing with other Norwegians, and that was difficult because I have a foreign diploma and foreign work experience.

In the beginning, I just sent my CV and cover letter without going there in person to present myself or call. I got no results. After a while, I became more proactive and started talking to the people in charge of each position I was applying for. However, I got the impression they wanted to hire someone who already had Norwegian work experience in that field.

How was Kulturkoordinator helpful in your job search?

In my situation, the problem was not that I was not being proactive, and I had the advantage of speaking the language. For me, what I needed was a personal coach who could help me understand a Norwegian interview and help prepare me for it. I had already done all the things that were necessary to get the interview. I was being proactive and showing initiative by going there and presenting myself in person.

However, I did not get the chance to go to any interviews because the competition for the available positions was high. So the moment when I finally got an interview, I thought; "Now it is important that I prepare myself on a very good level, so I feel well prepared and comfortable when going to the interview!"

Did the counselling work?

Yes, it worked, I got the job! One thing that I remember was that during the counselling, you (Ingrid) were asking me the interview questions in a much more profound way than what I would have prepared for myself.

You were especially digging into my personal motivation for the position. So for me it was about getting more confident, knowing what to expect from the interview, so that I could be relaxed and able to show them who I really am. It also helped to get the right words in Norwegian so that I could explain why it was my dream job. To talk about your motivation is an emotional thing, and it is harder to express when it is not your own language.

What was the hardest part about job seeking?

The frustration. Not knowing when or if I would succeed. Having this feeling of not being part of the society, and of not being able to contribute to the society. Not being able to get out of the house, and come back with more energy for my family. Moreover, the lack of intellectual input.

What was the best part about finding a job?

It made my days become more balanced. I am much happier now when I am at home, as a mom, than I was before. Of course, economically it also helps a lot. But the most important factor was the psychological factor. I became a bit of a different person after finding a job, I became happier as a person.

Sometimes while I was unemployed, I got frustrated. It was almost like depression I would say. I had periods where I felt really, really down. I think many other job seekers have a similar experience.

What would you advise other foreign job seekers to do?

Be proactive! Prepare yourself well before the interview. When I say proactive, I mean that you have to go to the company personally without an appointment, ask questions, and then write the cover letter afterwards. This is important. Also to learn the language, and try to get at least two Norwegian references, either as a volunteer or as something that is not in your work field. The important part is that they are Norwegian references.

Be well prepared for the interview because it is a situation where you are nervous, and you have to do it in another language and another country, so you need to build confidence that you are able to show your best assets and how you can contribute to the company.

CHAPTER FOURTEEN
START A BUSINESS

DAVID

If you are struggling to find a job or have an entrepreneurial spark, why not consider starting a business in Norway?

Whether you have dreams of building the next Facebook or just want to earn some freelance income on the side, starting a business is a popular option for foreigners, especially those who don't yet speak Norwegian.

The definition of business in Norway is far and wide. Earning money by selling home-made trinkets on Etsy, selling eBooks via Amazon, or selling advertising on a website that you run is all classed as business activity.

Anyone in Norway can earn up to 50,000 kroner per year from business activities without needing to formally register as a business. People falling into this category include hobbyists, and those offered the chance to present at a conference or to give a lecture at a university, for example. If you are intending to make money over the long-term, then you should register a business from day one regardless of the expected income.

Both Ingrid and I have run businesses in Norway, so we understand that this could be the right option for some people. Although this isn't a book on starting a business, I wanted to include some advice for those of you who might be considering it as an alternative to finding a job.

"My first work contacts were due to English connections in Oslo. Ironically, that's what helped me land my first employed job as a graphic designer. Some years later, I work as a freelance graphic designer in a collective studio in Oslo. While it's had its ups and downs, I've not looked back." - Tom Lenartowicz

BENEFITS OF STARTING A BUSINESS IN NORWAY

Registering a business in Norway is surprisingly easy. Unless you plan on starting a business that is particularly dangerous or needs licenses, you should be up and running within a week. Operating a business is also easier than in many other countries, with minimal paperwork required. Unless you plan on employing a lot of people, an accountant can probably take care of everything for you using just a couple of hours per month.

Starting a business is often an easy route to residency, most commonly for EU/EEA-citizens who just need to register their presence and complete a few forms. Of course, registering a business is one thing, but running a successful business over the long-term is something else entirely.

Another benefit is the relative honesty of how business is

conducted on time. Although there will always be some bad eggs, Norwegian customers tend to pay invoices on time and suppliers can generally be relied on.

Finally, registering as a freelancer can give you potential income while you search for a job. Not only can you work on freelance projects and build a portfolio while you look for jobs in your chosen field, you are also showcasing your skills and abilities in front of potential employers. Given the ease of registering for EU/EEA citizens, this is especially relevant for them.

DRAWBACKS OF STARTING A BUSINESS IN NORWAY

Working as a freelancer in Norway can be a tough slog. There is not much of a freelance or independent worker culture here as there are so many benefits of being employed. This means that many employers aren't used to working with freelancers. If you are building a business that's bigger than yourself, it can be difficult to break into the domestic market as a foreigner, especially if you can't yet speak Norwegian.

Although there isn't too much red tape, what there is can be difficult to deal with without a thorough knowledge of Norwegian law and financial terminology. Hiring professional help such as a bookkeeper, accountant, and legal counsel is strongly advised, but professional fees in Norway can be extremely high. You should figure on paying at least 750kr per hour for accountancy help and 2,000kr per hour for legal help.

The final drawback, cash flow, is a universal downside to starting a business and applies in most other countries. If you register as self-employed you will be expected to pay your expected tax in advance (more on this later), which can prove a hurdle too far in your first year or two.

BUSINESS EXAMPLES

Expats all over the world have set up successful businesses, often taking advantage of their unique perspectives or ties to their homeland. Here are some of the most popular tried and tested ideas that I have seen work in Norway.

Teaching your native language: More often associated with backpacking students, teaching languages is becoming a popular route to self-employment for many expats. Networking with existing language schools is a good way to start, as they may be able to offer you some contract work to get started.

The biggest downside of teaching English in Norway is that Norwegians are relatively fluent in English by the time they've left school, so the demand for qualified English teachers is much lower than in many other countries. However, the demand for teachers of other languages, particularly Spanish, is quite strong.

Translator: Related to the above, this is especially relevant if you can speak the language of your new country. But if you can speak two different languages, there's nothing to stop you from offering your services for that language pair online, to a global audience of billions. Just bear in mind that knowing two languages fluently does not make you a translator. Professional translators often specialise in a specific field such as science or finance, and often partner with one or more translation agencies to guarantee a regular source of clients.

Import/export: If you owned a business in your homeland, those connections could prove useful for establishing import/export links in Norway. It's a tough business though and you should conduct thorough market research before taking the plunge. For instance, are there any regulations you need to know about (this is particularly relevant to food), what are the tax implications, and is there a genuine market for your product beyond other expats? I've seen many businesses of this kind try and fail, and the biggest reason for failure was the market size was simply not big enough.

Café: Running cafes, restaurants and takeaways continue to be popular occupations for foreigners. Often influenced by cuisine from their homeland, these outlets can attract hungry locals as well as other expats. Location is critical and it's worth spending a lot of time in an area before committing to premises. Bear in mind that the Norwegian palate is not used to spicy, flavourful food of the kind served in Asia or Latin America, and you may need to "Norwegianise" your offer to find success here.

Tour guide: Expats are often employed as tour guides due to their native language ability, but why not take this a step further and offer personalised tours to visitors from your homeland? Remember to check with the local tourist office if you need a license.

Photography: If you are a skilled photographer then numerous opportunities exist for you to profit. But be warned, making the leap from keen amateur to professional is tougher than many people think. It's advisable to focus on a niche, for example serving corporate clients, weddings, wildlife or travel. If you're a prolific snapper, you could consider the growing micro-stock agency model. Or if you're more of a people person, why not offer photography workshops?

E-commerce: The internet has removed location as a barrier for many businesses, from digital service providers to webshops. It's now more common than you may think to source products and services from suppliers in Asia and sell to customers in America, all from the comfort of your home here in Europe. Many internet entrepreneurs get started by simply buying and selling on auction sites such as eBay, while services such as Fulfillment by Amazon have made it easier to progress to the next level. While e-commerce in Norway is popular, delivery charges are high and anything from abroad over a value of around 400kr attracts significant extra charges upon import. Bear this in mind if you are planning to import goods and sell them via a webshop here in Norway.

Virtual assistant: Do you have office administration or secretarial experience? Are you well organized and love helping people? Then you should consider the booming industry of virtual assistance. Smaller companies use VA's for a wide variety of tasks, such as bookkeeping, data entry, event planning and even web design. This saves them the overhead of an employee as they only need pay for work when they need it. By its very nature, VA work is remote, making it a great business choice for expats.

Of course, running such a business in Norway means you can't compete with some VA's who charge $10 per hour or less and expect to make a liveable wage. However, if you have some specific expertise that can command a premium rate, virtual assistance could be for you.

REGISTERING A BUSINESS

Almost anyone can register a business in Norway, but you must meet certain conditions if you want to use the business as a basis for residence. How strict those conditions are depends largely on your country of citizenship, the type of business you want to run, and your expected income. Below are the basics, but check the specifics for your own citizenship and circumstances with the Directorate of Immigration.

European citizens: EU/EEA citizens have a pretty easy time moving to Norway to work as a freelancer or self-employed individual. In most cases, to claim residency you simply turn up at your nearest Foreign Workers Service Centre or Police Station and fill out a few forms.

Citizens of other countries: Obtaining a residence permit by having your own business as a non-EU/EEA citizen is also possible, but the conditions are more onerous. First and foremost, you must be degree-educated or have undertaken vocational training that is directly relevant to your intended business.

You are limited to register as a sole proprietor, and must show proof of a likely income of at least 238,784kr per year. That is much lower than a typical Norwegian salary, but can still be a challenging figure to hit in year one of a business.

If your application is successful, you will be granted a one-year residence permit which can be renewed on an annual basis. After three years, you will be able to apply for a permanent residence permit.

Starting a side business: Many people who are employed full-time start a business on the side for some extra income. Before doing so, it's important to check with your employer if this is allowed. Even if your employment contract forbids it, some employers are fine with it as long as you ask first – and get the response in writing. If you are in Norway on a work permit linked to a specific job, check carefully because it's likely that this would also prevent you from starting a side business.

FORMS OF BUSINESS

One of the first decisions you need to make in your business plan is what corporate form to register. Here we outline the basic features of each, focusing on the main differences of personal rights and personal risk. For many entrepreneurs, the choice will be obvious, but for some you may need to consult with an accountant and/or lawyer.

ENK: Enkeltpersonforetak (Sole proprietorship)

The single-person business form is the cheapest and easiest business to start. The most important thing to understand about becoming a sole trader is that from both a tax and legal perspective, you and your business are one and the same. The business is taxed not as a separate entity but as part of your own overall income. Legally, with no separate entity you are personally liable if the business gets into trouble.

There is no need to run a payroll system to pay yourself. The profits of the business are yours to do with as you wish, which saves on bureaucracy. If you are good at managing money, this can be a big plus. If you are not good at managing your money, keep your business money at a distance, and pay yourself once a month to mimic a salary payment.

It's important to understand you are not classed as an employee, whether you do all the work yourself or employ others to work in the business. This means you receive less sickness benefit and do not qualify for unemployment benefits should your business fail, even though you pay a higher rate of social security.

You must pay your tax liability in advance four times a year. As this is based on expected income, this often causes cash-flow problems for new entrepreneurs, so be sure to fully understand this process before starting a sole proprietorship.

Cost: free to register, unless you are buying and selling goods, in which case the fees are 2250kr (online) or 2832kr (paper form)

Advantages: simple to understand, free to register, perfectly suitable for many small businesses and freelancers, no requirement to submit accounts or employ an auditor.

Disadvantages: full personal liability, tax payments in advance, may struggle to get credit, bigger customers may prefer to deal with limited companies.

AS: Aksjeselskap (Private Limited Liability Company)

A common form of business around the world, a limited liability company is a separate legal entity from its owners, thus limiting their personal liability. It can be owned by one or more people (shareholders) and the entity can own shares in other companies.

Shareholders can employ themselves in the business, making an AS suitable for a single-person business with high risk, or where the owner wants to increase social benefits.

The main disadvantages of forming an AS are the cost and added bureaucracy. In addition to the registration fee, a minimum of 30,000kr in share capital is required, which must be paid up front in cash or assets. That is the price of limited liability. The business requires a board of directors, and several formal documents are required. If the business has a turnover of above 5 million kroner in a year, the accounts must be formally audited.

Setting up a limited company is a serious business and it's highly advisable to employ the services of an accountant to advise you on initial formation at the very least.

Cost: Registration is 5,570kr (online) or 6,797kr (paper form). A minimum share capital of 30,000kr is also required.

Advantages: Limited liability for the owners, a respected form of company, possibility of credit, possible tax advantages.

Disadvantages: More expensive to setup and run, more statutory reporting, an accountant is highly advisable.

Other forms of business. With some online searching you'll come across references to norskregistrert utenlandsk foretak (NUF), which is a Norwegian branch of a foreign registered company. Up until a few years ago there were advantages to forming this kind of company, typically by registering a UK Limited company and then forming a Norwegian branch. But with recent easing of the ability to form an AS, many of these advantages are now non-existent.

If you are forming a business with others, you could also consider an Ansvarlig Selskap (ANS/DA), which is a partnership agreement most commonly used in law and accountancy practices. The General Partnership is similar to a sole proprietorship, with ownership shared by two or more people. Partners cannot be employed in the business so retain the "self-employed" characteristics of the sole proprietorship, however there are more formalities.

There are two forms of general partnership, ANS and DA. The key difference is liability. Within an ANS, each partner is jointly liable and can be pursued for all debts of the partnership, whereas within a DA, each partner is liable only for the percentage agreed upon in a partnership agreement.

Which business form is right for you? We can't answer that question, as it depends entirely on you, your own personal financial circumstances, your ambition for the business, your attitude to risk, and many other factors. If you are a single person testing out an idea, then registering as a sole proprietor is probably the best idea. It allows you to get up and running quickly with minimal bureaucracy, and you can always convert to a Limited Company later.

Of course, if you are a non-EU/EEA citizen registering a business in order to obtain a residence permit, the choice is made for you. You must register a sole proprietorship.

OPERATING A BUSINESS

This is a book about finding a job and not running a business, so we are not going to dwell too much on the ins and outs of running a business. However, some of you will be considering going down this road so it's important to make sure you understand the obligations you will have.

Firstly, invoicing rules are strict. Drawing up a quick invoice in Word won't cut it in Norway. An electronic invoicing system that can be audited is an essential investment, and an accountant is highly recommended even if you have the simplest of businesses.

Once you've invoiced a total of 50,000kr to Norwegian clients, you are required to register for merverdiavgift (MVA), which the Norwegian version of value-added tax. This is a 25% tax added to the cost of most goods and services, which you are then required to report and submit to the government. The law on this tax can be complex and strict regulations are in place, so talk to an accountant to understand your obligations or you'll face a hefty fine.

There are some insurance policies you are required to have, and others you should consider. If you have employees, workers' compensation insurance is mandatory, as is having an occupational pension scheme. Disability insurance, life insurance, travel insurance, and fire and theft insurance should also be considered.

Useful resources:

- Norwegian Directorate of Immigration: https://www.udi.no/
- Brønnøysund Register Centre: https://www.brreg.no/

CHAPTER FIFTEEN
FINAL THOUGHTS

We hope that by reading this book you are now better prepared for the job search process ahead of you. If you've already been struggling to find employment, you should now have a toolkit to improve your chances and a roadmap to securing that all important job.

"Be patient. Finding work in Norway is a process. Be prepared for no answers and absolutely no replies. I must have sent over 80 applications and it sometimes felt as if I was really stuck. Keeping busy and having a good daily routine that combines searching online or in person is key. My first job was looking for employment but I also spent a lot of time walking in the woods to unwind. Exercise helps you stay positive and reduces the anxiety of not having found work. Job agencies can get you working faster and lead to full time opportunities or help you gain valuable local experience. I took a temp job in order to show relevant work experience in Norway. This led to more interesting opportunities further down the road." - James M. Miller

---

Before we sign off, we want to repeat some of the most important pieces of advice from the book:

Be clear about what you want and what you have to offer.

Commit to learning Norwegian.

Build a personal network by meeting as many relevant people (in Norwegian!) as possible.

If you're not yet in Norway, try to make connections on social media such as LinkedIn, but remember, nothing beats an in-person meeting.

And above all: don't give up!

Our very best wishes,

- Ingrid & David

Life in Norway

Expat website and podcast

www.lifeinnorway.net

Norway Weekly

The essential email newsletter

www.lifeinnorway.net/weekly

Moon Norway

Travel guidebook & trip planning advice

www.lifeinnorway.net/moon

35797436R00083

Printed in Great Britain
by Amazon